LIVING MIRACLES

The Spiritual Sons of John Paul the Great

RANDALL J. MEISSEN, LC

MissionNetwork

Alpharetta, Georgia

Published by Mission Network Programs USA, Inc.

CIP Data is on file with the Library of Congress

ISBN 978-1-933271-27-9

PRINTED IN THE UNITED STATES OF AMERICA

8 7 6 5 4 3 2 1

FIRST EDITION

Dedicated with Gratitude

to the Salisbury Knights of Columbus

Pius XII Council, No. 4679

Who once gave a grade-school boy

the first Bible of his own

TABLE OF CONTENTS

FOREWORD

Simon, son of John, do you love me?
John 21:17

Throughout his long pontificate, John Paul the Great urged Catholics again and again to take up the task of a "new evangelization" of the world. That work belongs to every Catholic, but especially to priests. In the words of Vatican II, ". . . since nobody can be saved who has not first believed, it is the first task of priests as coworkers of bishops to preach the Gospel of God to all [men and women]" (PO, 4).

And because no one can give what he does not have himself, the council urged priests to "immerse themselves in Scripture by constant sacred reading and diligent study" (DV, 25). Priests, like their people, need to encounter Jesus Christ through Word and sacrament – and just as God's Word became flesh in Jesus Christ, so every priest, configured to Christ through ordination, should strive to be God's Word *becoming* flesh in the life of his people.

Today, the Church across the United States and the developed world faces a new kind of mission territory, a vast array of pastoral challenges. We live in a time of great material success and scientific self-assurance, but where the inner life is withering, private spiritualities replace communities of real faith, and loneliness is the daily routine of millions.

Faced with these realities, the Church has no room for men who see the priesthood as a privileged caste; or an easy job; or an escape from the world; or a safe harbor for their personal confusions; or an avenue for their ambition.

Rather, God calls and the Church needs *heroes:* priests who love God more than themselves; who seek God's glory more than their own; who want to lead by serving others; who have a mercy and humility born of a knowledge of their own sins; who have the courage to preach the truth even in the face of contempt; who have a hunger for winning souls; priests who are faithful to the Church and her teachings; who are obedient to their vocation as Jesus Christ was obedient to his; who stand *in persona Christi* – modeling the person of Christ to their people.

In the years ahead, the priests we need are men who will turn away from comfort, who will listen for the voice of God, who will follow Jesus Christ into the storm, and in their failures, will turn to him.

We need a new Pentecost. We need priests who are men of prayer, men of courage, men for others, men anchored in the sacramental life of the Church. We need priests who will spark not a new clericalism, but a new friendship, equality, cooperation, and fire from every vocation and form of discipleship in the Church.

We need priests who can answer generously and honestly *yes* when Jesus asks them, "Simon, son of John, do you love me?"

God is calling these men right now – in the witness and personal testimonies of Brother Meissen's book, and in a hundred other ways every day. They are already among us. And beginning today, there is no more important task for every parent, every teacher, every friend, and every pastor to find them, support them, encourage them, and urge them forward to accept God's gift.

+Charles J. Chaput, O.F.M. Cap.
Archbishop of Denver

INTRODUCTION

Now more than ever it is crucial that you be "watchers of the dawn," the lookouts who announce the light of dawn and the new springtime of the Gospel of which the buds can already be seen.

Pope John Paul II[1]

Twilight Flows to Dawn

"Are you praying for John Paul?"

The shouted question caught my attention, and I glanced over my shoulder, catching sight of its unlikely source. A young man, not more than nineteen, stood at the street-side newsstand, bedecked with black leather, tattoos, dyed hair, and all. He was a teenage hybrid of goth and grunge, quite a contrast to the long, winding column processing past him along the New York street.

The passing Eucharistic procession must have puzzled the young man. The scene was almost surreal, like a picture from a medieval manuscript. First came a tall wooden cross held high, and far behind, a canopy carried aloft by four poles, beneath which a priest, resplendent in ornate vestments, bore the Blessed Sacrament encased in a sunburst monstrance of shimmering gold. Between the cross and the canopy came the faithful, row after row, chanting and singing, many arrayed in religious garb: seminarians in black cassocks, friars in earthen brown and smoky grey, Mother Teresa's missionary sisters in white saris fringed with blue, and many more.

This day was April's first, but the sheer size and solemnity of the marching company dispelled any suspicion of jest. In fact, the event had been planned long in advance. The Pope himself had sent the magnificent monstrance which led the procession through the streets of New York. Yet no one in the archdiocese, not even the cardinal, could have planned the affair to take place on such a day. Providence alone knew that this April day in 2005 would be the eve before the Pontiff's passing.

Front pages on the newsstand racks already carried images of a failing pope. News anchors and commentators all agreed that his condition was grave. And it *was* grave, mortally grave. Nonetheless, as John Paul slipped into final sleep, he worked a miracle; for at that dingy New York newsstand along the urban street an unlikely young man's heart, beating beneath black leather, was pierced by the final witness of a saint.

The simple question, "Are you praying for John Paul?" was genuine, filled with empathy and respect. It was a question that touched me deeply. Was I praying for John Paul? I paused for an instant, standing there, myself among the cassock-clad seminarians, and responded, "Yes." Yes indeed, I prayed for John Paul II, because he had changed my life.

Twice prior, I had been the inquisitive young man standing stunned on the roadside. The first time, I stood in the dark of night along a Houston highway, staring at a smashed wreck and a dead friend. In that moment, I was the one asking questions. Why had it happened this way? Why had I been spared? Standing there, looking at my selfish life and its shattered ambitions, I knew the reason. God had given me another chance; he had given me the chance to walk where he led, if I but had the courage to respond and the courage to hope. Thus I offered Christ my life and started down his path.

The second time, I stood along a Roman road. Four months had passed since the Houston crash, and it was June of 2000's Great Jubilee. On the eve of Corpus Christi, I beheld a procession even more remarkable than the one in New York, for it was attended by scores of scarlet-robed cardinals and bishops in violet, and in its midst was John Paul II himself. With excitement, I craned my neck to see the Pope as he passed only a few meters away. Then something extraordinary happened – *he looked at me.*

Time and again, I have heard that experience repeated by others. Amid great crowds, at his audiences and at World Youth Days, at Masses and celebrations, John Paul II had the ability to look through the droves of people and to penetrate an individual's soul. I never would have given the account credence had I not also experienced the force of his glance. There in Rome, beyond the ancient Basilica of John Lateran, on the feast of Corpus Christi, the Pope saw through a formless crowd and with piercing gaze looked at *me.* In his deep eyes, filled with purity and peace, I saw the priest I wanted to be.

I saw a man who had given everything, a man so completely identified with Christ that he could rightly say, "I have been crucified with Christ; it is no longer I who live, but Christ who lives in me."[2] In him, I and many others saw more than an aged sage; we saw more than a famous figure or a media personality. We saw more than just John Paul II, for he was, in a sense, more than himself. He was the Lord's Vicar.

I looked into his eyes, and I saw Christ.

I saw the one who, noticing a short man struggling to catch sight of him, "looked up and spoke to him, 'Zacchaeus, come down.'"[3] I saw the one who "turned and looked straight at Peter"[4] evoking a tearful flood of repentance. I saw the one who looked steadily at a rich young man and "was filled with love for him, and said, 'You need to do one thing more.'"[5]

I looked into his eyes, and I saw Christ.

I was the one who needed to do one thing more.

That experience is what motivated me to write this book. I am convinced that my story is not isolated, because I have so often heard it repeated by young people, by other seminarians, and among priests. John Paul II was not a distant pope; rather, he was always spiritually and often physically close to his flock. He strove to be a paternal presence.

My generation of Catholics, and more, live in John Paul's shadow. Growing up as a Missouri farm boy, I knew no other pope. Only a month after I was born, his papal white was splashed with red by the bullet of a would-be assassin. By the time I was in middle school, the word "pope" was simply synonymous with "John Paul II." My older cousins spoke of seeing him at World Youth Day in Denver; my high school friends enthusiastically recounted their "close encounter" when he visited St. Louis in 1999—a visit on which the Pope persuaded our governor to stop a scheduled execution. Even as far off as I was from the beaten path, way out in the boondocks of rural America, John Paul II never seemed distant.

Certainly, my experience, despite its particularities, is not wholly unique. More than an entire generation came to maturity under the reign of John Paul II. If he was an earthquake, then the youth, ever near his heart, were at its epicenter. My time studying for the priesthood has only confirmed this sentiment. John Paul II has touched my brother seminarians as deeply as he touched me. Some even cite a direct encounter with him as the moment of their priestly call. These and many others, continue to see him as a model and a spiritual father.

For us, John Paul II is an example of courage, of sacrifice, and of hope. His example is acute because he wrestled with the same call as us, the call to serve Christ in holy priesthood. We looked to John Paul for strength while discerning God's call amid a hostile culture. We looked to him when the question, "Who am I and what does God want me to be?" shook us to the core.

John Paul II never concealed the challenge that embracing a priestly vocation poses. In his final "Message to the Youth of the World" he acknowledged, "Listening to Christ and worshiping him leads us to make *courageous choices*, to take what are sometimes heroic decisions."[6] The priestly vocation is a path which demands a heroic change of direction in the life of a young man – sometimes even a full U-turn!

Yet John Paul assured us that Christ traveled the same road of sacrifice long ago, sandal-shod, dragging a cross of timber, and he returns to travel it again at our side. For that reason, fear of suffering and the cross cannot cause those called by Christ to sell themselves short, to pass up their chance for genuine happiness. John Paul witnessed this truth with his words and his life. For my generation, his white-clad likeness is forever emblazoned upon our vision of the priesthood.

Therefore, I have come to believe that many young priests and seminarians who trace their vocation, the origin of their priestly call, to John Paul's reign of hope bear the special stamp of his influence. Among the ranks of young men who were called to Christ's service, who entered the seminary, and who were ordained to the priesthood during his reign, are found the spiritual sons of John Paul the Great. They are his lasting legacy, his living miracles.

Chapter 1
THE MOUNTAINS

An Uphill Battle

Father Ed Kelly, being born and raised in the city of Philadelphia, was never much of an outdoorsman. The closest he came to nature was mowing the small plot of grass in front of the house, imaginatively called a front lawn. Sure, some Boy Scout might get a kick out of traipsing off through the woods on his weekends, foraging for food, and then curling up on a rock for the night, but most normal people would prefer to get their dose of nature by popping a slice of pizza into the microwave and sitting down with a copy of *National Geographic.* Lugging a hiker's pack of gear up the side of a cliff was definitely not Father Kelly's idea of fun.

But people change.

Father Kelly had been a priest for three years when, on November 10, 1993, he concelebrated Mass with Pope John Paul II. Every detail about that morning is carved into his mind. He can still see the Pope standing at the altar as though it were yesterday. There was something unique and compelling about the way John Paul celebrated Mass. He never went carelessly through the motions – rather, every word was spoken purposefully, and every gesture and motion was attentive and deliberate, offered as a prayer of supplication to the Father. The way that John Paul celebrated Mass pierced Father Kelly's heart.

Father Kelly was an enthusiastic young priest. He was faithful to his duties, he prayed his daily prayers, and he strove to treat others with kindness. Yet deep down he knew that God was asking for something more. There were already enough "good men" in the world; God needed his priests to be men of extreme holiness, men willing to become saints.

The experience of concelebrating Mass with the Pope sparked what Father Kelly calls his "second conversion." Thereafter, he began intensely reading everything he could get his hands on related to John Paul II: his encyclicals, his books, his speeches and homilies, and biographies written about him. From his reading, Father Kelly soon realized that John Paul's holiness was not an accident. It came from a lifetime of effort, from love purified in the face of suffering, from choosing day after day to climb the narrow path marked out by God. Father Kelly realized that to become the priest God wanted him to be, he needed to start climbing.

"Mountains are a great symbol for the spiritual and ethical life," says Father Kelly. "Climbing up a mountain is difficult." The analogy is easy to grasp because mountains always present a challenge. It demands effort, struggle, and sweat to reach the summit of a towering peak. No one can get to the top by taking it easy, by coasting along and strolling lazily across the level plain. Only a determined climber can scale to the top. Only he can taste the cool, clean mountain air and behold the beauty of the valley below.

The fact that Jesus Christ himself often went up a mountain to pray underscores the image. From the summit he conversed with his Father, enveloped in solitude and surrounded by creation's majesty. Atop lofty Mount Tabor he revealed his divine glory to Peter and the sons of Zebedee, and from humble Calvary's crest he revealed the glory of his cross.

Now Father Kelly takes the symbolism of mountains seriously. He views each day as a challenge, as a chance to scale a little higher in the spiritual life. He also has started imitating a more superficial aspect of John Paul's example by making the decision to take up mountaineering himself. "I figured that if the Pope could climb mountains, then I could too," he says.

In one of his more daring trips, Father Kelly set out to find the mountain chalet where John Paul was accustomed to stay during his pontifical mountain excursions. After hiking back and forth in the mountains of Northern Italy's Valle d'Aosta region, searching endlessly for the small lodge, Father Kelly finally succeeded. His search was worth the struggle, for from the picnic table outside the Pope's cabin he beheld a spectacular, breathtaking view of Mount Blanc.

Call of the Mountains

Karol Wojtyla had the mountains in his blood. Something about them was irresistible; their grandeur, their beauty, and their challenging heights called to him. As a priest, he often spent his vacations hiking in the Bieszczady Mountains and canoeing on the nearby lakes.

Karol was on just such a trip in July of 1958 when he was summoned by the Primate of Poland, Cardinal Stefan Wyszynski. The cardinal informed Karol that he had been named a bishop. At first, Karol feared that as a bishop he would be unable to continue his customary summer excursions. However, he need not have worried, for he was able to continue them until 1978, when he donned a new name and a white cassock.[7]

Taking the office of pope entailed many sacrifices: departure from his Polish homeland, separation from trusted companions, and abandoning the Bieszczady Mountains. Still, John Paul II would not be a prisoner of the Vatican. Even as Pope, he occasionally escaped to go hiking in Italy's Eastern Alps, and Cardinal Stanislaw Dziwisz, John Paul's longtime secretary, recounts that in the early years of the pontificate, they smuggled the Pope out of the Vatican in plainclothes on over a hundred occasions to go skiing. Remarkably, no one recognized him – but of course, who would ever have suspected that the Pope went skiing?

Perhaps the mountains helped draw John Paul II to Denver in 1993. No doubt, the towering Rockies appealed to his youthful heart, and their imposing peaks provided a perfect backdrop for World Youth Day, an ideal destination for a flood of young pilgrims. "Upon arriving in Denver," the Holy Father commented, "I lifted up my eyes towards the splendor of the Rocky Mountains whose majesty and power recall that all our help comes from the Lord who has made heaven and earth. He alone is the *rock of our salvation.*"[8]

The Mountains and Good-Looking Girls

The mountains certainly brought nineteen-year-old Peter Mitchell to Denver. Peter accompanied his church youth group to World Youth Day, but seeing the Pope was not his primary objective. "There were two reasons I went," he notes. "God roped me in through the mountains and some good-looking girls."

Now, whenever Father Peter Mitchell gives talks to young people, he always jokes about not being sold on the idea of going on a church trip to see the Pope. However, he knew they were going to go hiking in the Rocky Mountains, and he loved the mountains. Also, there were some girls going on the trip that he really liked, so he naturally wanted to accompany them. The future priest never expected what Denver held in store for him; he was in for far more than he bargained.

Seeing Pope John Paul II, witnessing his zeal, his love, and his boldness in proclaiming the Gospel was a turning point in Father Peter's life. He was transformed from living his faith in an ashamed and sheepish kind of way. He left with a bold desire to proclaim the Gospel and to share his faith with others. Father Peter looks at the opening ceremony of World Youth Day in Denver's Mile High Stadium as a Pentecost moment in his own life, a moment where he felt and experienced the awesome force of the Holy Spirit. For the first time, Father Peter saw the church as something alive, vibrant, and very powerful. That was a gift worth sharing with others.

Such is also the case with many priests of his generation. Many were either at World Youth Day in Denver or influenced by that event in some other way. Denver remains a benchmark that they look back to as the moment when they were sent forth on a mission by the Pope himself.

Roots of a Vocation

Father Peter grew up in a good Catholic family in Milwaukee, Wisconsin. He credits his parents for giving him a solid foundation in the faith, and he is grateful to the parish priests who gave him good examples to follow, especially those involved with his parents in the charismatic renewal. As a child, he greatly admired those priests. Consequently, he thought about the priesthood while still a small boy, even mentioning that interest to his parents.

Nonetheless, by his teenage years, he had placed his interest in the priesthood on the back burner. He still went to church with his family and stayed somewhat involved, but he also was very enamored by the prevalent culture of the time. Catholicism was not cool. Gradually, he became unsure and somewhat embarrassed about the Catholic faith.

But that was before he encountered John Paul II. World Youth Day in Denver is the event that divides Father Peter's life in two. He has a vivid memory of the opening welcome ceremony in Mile High Stadium on Thursday, August 12, 1993. Although he did not recognize it as such at the time, Father Peter believes that John Paul II's arrival was accompanied by an overwhelming outpouring of the Holy Spirit upon the gathered crowd.

"The experience of being in the Holy Father's presence totally blew me away," Father Peter recalls. "As soon as he entered the stadium that day, everyone around me, including myself, started crying, and no one could really explain why. It was just so powerful, so beautiful – the Holy Father's love and his joy and his presence."

Clouds Clearing

Torrential rains welcomed John Paul to Denver, but the downpour did not dampen his spirits. Undaunted by the inclement weather, the Holy Father greeted his youthful crowd with an explosive message.

"Young people of America and of the world, listen to what Christ the Redeemer is saying to you! 'To all who received him, who believed in his name, he gave power to become children of God.' The World Youth Day challenges you to be fully conscious of who you are as God's dearly beloved sons and daughters.[9]

"Jesus has called each one of you to Denver for a purpose: You must live these days in such a way that, when the time comes to return home, each one of you will have a clearer idea of what Christ expects of you. Each one must have the courage to go and spread the Good News … among young people of your own age, who will take the church and society into the next century."[10]

Father Peter remembers how hard it was raining while the Pope delivered these words. It poured rain, and the Pope spoke, and it kept raining. Father Peter's youth group was waving Vatican flags amid the rain, and they all were soaking wet. As the ceremony concluded, the Holy Father invited everyone to join in praying the Our Father in Latin. When they began, something extraordinary happened.

"The biggest rainbow you've ever seen came over the stadium as we sang the Pater Noster," Father Peter recounts. "It was the most remarkable, dramatic convergence of the elements – a total theophany. At that moment, as the Pope is singing the Our Father, the rain stops and this beautiful, perfect rainbow appears directly over the stadium. It could have had a pot of gold at the end. It was amazing, and everyone who was there remembers that."

The youth pilgrimage was on Saturday, August 14. Subsequent World Youth Days have greatly scaled down this pilgrimage component due to logistical concerns, but at Denver the youth made a fifteen-mile long trek from downtown Denver to Cherry Creek State Park in sweltering heat. Father Peter recalls it as a physically grueling experience. "I'm a good athlete, I ran track and I run marathons, but even for me, carrying all my gear on that pilgrimage hike was intense. We were in the mountains, the sun was hot, and we were exhausted. We didn't have enough water, and some people collapsed of heat exhaustion." When the young people arrived at Cherry Creek State Park, they joined the Pope for an evening prayer vigil.

The closing Mass for World Youth Day was the next morning, on the Feast of the Assumption of Mary. Often, when he gives youth talks, Father Peter looks back at John Paul II's homilies and addresses in Denver. The Pope spoke about proclaiming the Gospel from the rooftops, and urged his listeners to be proud to be Catholic. Father Peter recounts, "He still had so much vigor back then that he spoke very dramatically and forcefully. He really challenged us to be bold witnesses to Christ in the public square."

In that closing homily, John Paul II appealed directly to the youth:

> *"The Church needs your energies, your enthusiasm, your youthful ideals, in order to make the Gospel of Life penetrate the fabric of society, transforming people's hearts and the structures of society in order to create a civilization of true justice and love. Now more than ever, in a world that is often without light and without the courage of noble ideals, people need the fresh, vital spirituality of the Gospel.*
>
> *'Do not be afraid to go out on the streets and into public places, like the first apostles who preached Christ and the Good News of salvation in the squares of cities, towns, and villages. This is no time to be ashamed of the Gospel.*[11] *It is the time to preach it from the rooftops.*[12] *Do not be afraid to break out of comfortable and routine modes of living, in order to take up the challenge of making Christ known in the modern 'metropolis.' It is you who must 'go out into the byroads'*[13] *and invite everyone you meet to the banquet which God has prepared for his people. The Gospel must not be kept hidden because of fear or indifference. It was never meant to be hidden away in private. It has to be put on a stand so that people may see its light and give praise to our heavenly Father.'"*[14]

By the time the Mass concluded, Father Peter was physically and spiritually exhausted. "We were very tired, and it was hot," Father Peter remembers, "I fell asleep for part of the

Mass because I was so exhausted." Some of this exhaustion was likely playing into the mixture, but when the Holy Father gave his final blessing, Father Peter was deeply moved: "I knelt down in the dirt there and started crying. I had been resisting my vocation for a long time, just kind of interiorly fighting it, and denying it, and saying I didn't have to be a priest despite knowing from the time that I was very little that I was being called. I really stopped resisting on that day, and said, 'Alright, I'm going to do whatever the Lord wants.'" The moment of Father Peter's actual entrance into the seminary came later, but the moment when his wall of interior resistance came crumbling down was on his knees there at World Youth Day.

Closure

Ten years later, Father Peter again knelt for the Holy Father's blessing, but this time it was on the polished marble floor of the Apostolic Palace at the Vatican, and he was close enough to kiss the Pope's hand in gratitude. Father Peter was studying in Rome as a priest when his bishop arranged for him to meet John Paul II personally in the Vatican. "I got the call the night before and was all excited," Father Peter remembers. "I wondered what to say to the Pope, knowing that I would only have about ten seconds to speak." The meeting took place in the Pope's private library between the routine reception of various foreign dignitaries.

Father Peter thought for a long time about what he would say. He went through all sorts of different scenarios before he decided. At last, as he knelt before the Pope, he said, "Holy Father, I was in Denver."

The pope replied inquisitively, "Denver?"

Father Peter added, "At World Youth Day."

The Pope nodded and said in a deep voice, "I remember."

Father Peter continued, "I listened to you, and I became a priest."

The Pope answered, "Very good!" He imparted his blessing, making the sign of the cross over Father Peter's head, and gave him a rosary as a gift.

A picture of that moment hangs proudly on Father Peter's rectory wall. "After having been one of the kids out there in the crowd at Denver," comments Father Peter, "I was blessed to be able to tell John Paul that he was the reason I became a priest. I was so proud to tell him that he was my father, that I had listened to him, and that I had done what he asked of us. That meeting was a beautiful gift from our Lord. Still when I look at the picture, I can't believe it really happened."

The Heart of a Priest

Now Father Peter tries to imbue his priestly ministry with the "JP II spirit." He is pastor of a small rural parish, and commutes to teach classes at the diocesan seminary. John Paul II's model of youth ministry is something he consciously imitates by reaching out to the youth, listening to them, and spending time with them. He sees his work with young people as a ministry of presence, so he makes a point of going to their track meets and basketball games to reach them where they are.

Father Peter also helps coach track at the public school in town several days a week. "I'm a runner," he says, "and I try to be involved in athletics. I see that as an important way of fulfilling my duty as a priest. I want to show them that being a priest is being fully a man, being fully alive, and fully involved in life."

Father Peter has filled the walls of his rectory with pictures of John Paul II. He has photos of the Pope as a young priest, pictures of him skiing in the mountains and kayaking down rivers. He has later photos too, images of the Pope with young people, pictures from international trips and World Youth Days. "Many of the kids don't really remember John Paul," Father Peter notes. "Some didn't know him at all, and if they did know him it was as an old man. I try to show them his example of loving life and living it to the full."

Old-fashioned fun is mixed with formal catechesis at Father Peter's weekly youth group meetings. Bonfires, pilgrimages, and canoe trips are part of their curriculum. When I spoke with Father Peter, he was finalizing arrangements for a youth pilgrimage to Rome. Nearly a year of preparation went into the trip, and twenty-eight enthused high school teenagers were signed up to go. "I'm really excited that it's all come together and that the Lord's made this possible," Father Peter said, "We are going to pray at John Paul's tomb, and all these kids are going to have a pretty intense experience of faith."

In his role as pastor, Father Peter seeks to engage his parishioners in such a way that they will encounter and speak with the Lord. In his view, every priest is charged with bringing the Gospel alive. The best way to achieve this is by living liturgical life to the full as the Second Vatican Council envisioned its renewal. "Pope John Paul II truly understood and saw the potential of the Council to renew every aspect of the life of the Church," says Father Peter. "World Youth Day was just one manifestation of that renewed vibrant liturgical and spiritual life."

Father Peter wants the faith to intersect the real lives of his parishioners. Simple things like walking down the street wearing a Roman collar help him to engage people. If there is a big town event, like the annual Fourth of July parade, Father Peter will be there, shaking hands and mingling with the crowd. He sees such behavior as nothing extraordinary because every priest must relate to people where they are by taking interest in their interests.

"I think this gets a little deep here," Father Peter reflects. "Talking about John Paul II's phenomenology is not something I do on an everyday basis with the people in my country parish. Since they are not studying philosophy, it may not be so important that they understand what it is in itself. But the basic idea is simple. Every person has value, and therefore the life of every individual has great meaning and dignity."

That is why Father Peter thinks it is important occasionally to go out harvesting with the farmers, to learn about hog farming, and to help with the volunteer fire department.

These activities are part of daily life for his parishioners, and they are the places where men and women who are fully alive can be touched by Jesus. "My role as priest, as preacher, and as minister of the sacraments is to bring Jesus into the lives of every person," Father Peter says.

John Paul II nobly demonstrated how Christ is able to enter into all the aspects of ordinary life and elevate their meaning. His personal relationship with Christ vivified all dimensions of his day. Father Peter says, "I know that many of my peers as diocesan priests understand that our biggest priority is to be men of prayer, men of Eucharistic adoration, men who are faithful to confession, who have devotion to Mary, and who live in fidelity to the Magisterium. In those ways we are formed by Christ through his Bride the church, and our relationship with the Lord is the source and spiritual center of all we do. What we give to others comes from our relationship with Christ."

A Hope-Filled Future

Because of his interaction with diocesan seminarians and priests, Father Peter has great hope for the future of the church. Part of that is due to what he calls the "JP II generation." During his years of study, Father Peter spent time at St. Charles Seminary in Philadelphia and at the North American College in Rome. Now he knows priests across the country who share his passion and admiration for John Paul II.

This makes Father Peter very optimistic. "All the problems in the world and in the church today could make you very discouraged, negative, and frustrated. But John Paul II always exuded a joyful confidence which came from his love for the Lord and his faith in Jesus. Today, I see that vocations are flourishing, youth ministry is thriving, and young people are living the sacramental life in places where they encounter young priests and religious on fire with love for the Lord."

Father Peter has had the opportunity to be present at many of John Paul II's visits and World Youth Days. In those circumstances, he sees himself, within his sphere of pastoral ministry, as mirroring John Paul II's priestly witness. He wants to show the young people that he understands them. "The priests who go to World Youth Day have a common experience," Father Peter says, "They want to go despite the difficulty and exhaustion it entails. There is an uplifting experience that comes from accompanying the youth. It reminds us that we are also on a pilgrimage to God, and I think it permits us to remain young at heart."

FATHER ED KELLY *is a priest in the Archdiocese of Philadelphia, Pennsylvania.*

FATHER PETER MITCHELL *is a priest in the diocese of Lincoln, Nebraska, and has the rare privilege of serving under his onetime parish pastor, Bishop Fabian Bruskewitz. He is the author of* John Paul II, We Love You: Young People Encounter the Pope *(Servant Publications: Ann Arbor, Michigan).*

Chapter 2
KITCHENS AND CUPS

Midnight Snack

As midnight drew near on January 26, 1979, the first day of John Paul II's historic visit to Mexico, each passing moment engraved the day's events more deeply into sleepyheads. By taking his first pastoral trip abroad, less than four months after his election, the Polish Pontiff set the tone for a new style of papacy: John Paul II would not be a "prisoner" of the Vatican; rather, he would go out to the world and meet its people where they were – both geographically and spiritually. He had a great sympathy for Mexico, a nation whose overwhelmingly Catholic populace, much like Poland's, had suffered tremendously at the hands of anti-Catholic and anticlerical oppressors.

This day of the visit had been exhausting, even for him. From the moment he stepped down from his plane to kiss the Mexican soil, he was met by a hurricane of activity. The president of the Republic – despite stipulating that the Pope would not be received as a head of state – decided to greet him at the airport with an "unofficial" welcome. President José López Portillo's decision was, without doubt, inspired by the deluge of enthusiasm that the Pope's visit had generated among the Mexican populace. More than a million people would, in fact, line the streets to welcome the Pope as the papal entourage made its way from the airport into Mexico City.

The day's agenda was only beginning. The Pope had to celebrate Mass in the cathedral, address the 300,000 Mexicans gathered in Constitution Square, and meet the president's family together with an endless stream of churchmen and dignitaries. Activity followed activity in ceaseless succession, and the Pope scarcely had time to catch his breath. Concerns over his address in a few days to the Latin American Bishops Conference in Puebla on January 28th – an address with enormous consequences for the future of Catholicism in Latin America[15] – must have weighed heavily on his mind as well.

When "day one" reached an end, the Holy Father, his staff, a few Mexican priests, and selected members of the organizing committee withdrew to the residence of Archbishop Girolamo Prigione, the Holy See's apostolic delegate to Mexico, for some well-deserved rest. This arrangement set the stage for an unexpected rendezvous.

Álvaro Corcuera, a Mexican consecrated member of the Regnum Christi movement who was assisting with the organization of the trip, scarcely twenty years old at the time, was among the privileged few lodging at the residence. His day had been exhilarating; he was living out a page of history. But as the whirlwind of work came to an end late that night, Álvaro's attention was caught by a rumbling noise. His stomach was growling; he was hungry! So he ventured into the kitchen.

Just as Álvaro was about to take a bite to eat, the door swung open, and an all-too-familiar figure dressed in white stepped in. It was the Pope. They were soon joined by a third person, a Mexican priest. With snacks in hand, this unexpected trio conversed into the early morning hours about the Church, the faith of the Mexican people, and the continued work of catechesis and evangelization throughout the country. Álvaro expected the Holy Father to be tired and eager to rest after his long day, but instead the Holy Father was more interested in the spiritual welfare of his flock in Mexico.

Finally, the Holy Father asked where the chapel was, and there he remained for quite some time before retiring to his room for a few hours of rest. By five o'clock in the morning, a huge crowd, hoping for a quick glimpse of the Pope, had amassed outside the apostolic delegate's residence. John Paul II soon appeared at the window with his breviary in hand and said: "I will greet you in half an hour. The Pope must first pray. He will have nothing to give you if he doesn't pray."

These two incidents left a profound first impression on his young kitchen companion. John Paul II had a hunger that no food could satisfy; his love for Christ and his impassioned desire for the salvation of souls drove him to sacrifice himself without limit. Yet this same hunger for Christ and souls also drove the Pope to prayer. John Paul II knew that his actions alone would not suffice; he had to pray. He found his rest, strength, and inspiration in prayer.

The young man also found that he shared the Pope's hunger. He is now a priest: Father Álvaro Corcuera, general director of a religious congregation, the Legionaries of Christ. Father Álvaro recalls: "My first encounter with John Paul II was in a kitchen; I would have wanted it to be in a beautiful cathedral, but no, it was in a kitchen… despite that, I was – and always will be – struck by his deep and loving gaze. You could see that John Paul II was a true man of prayer, an apostle. The Pope changed the world because all that he did, he first heard and received in prayer. We must follow the Pope's example. We too, must believe in the power of prayer, ceaseless prayer."

Awakening

Ever since he was a child, Stephen Savel wanted to join the army. He was probably one of those imaginative kids for whom every stick was a gun, every toy car a battle tank, and every bush a camouflaged invader. As soon as he got the chance, he joined the "Cadets," the Canadian youth organization for aspiring soldiers. Later he entered the army reserve and started training on weekends. At last, when he was old enough, he traveled to Britain and joined the army there.

He wanted to see the world, to do something meaningful, to stand up courageously in defense of freedom. He never expected his term of service to be a time of spiritual awakening. "I wasn't from an overly strong Catholic family," he admits. "In fact, the only time I can recall praying as a kid was before hockey games or when my grandparents were present for family meals."

But God draws straight with crooked lines. During his military service, Stephen was away from his family and friends for the first time, and almost unconsciously he started praying more. When everyone else was far away, he began to realize that God was near. Also, a zealous priest in Scotland went out of his way to make him feel welcome, while at the same time Stephen was confronted for the first time in his life with serious anti-Catholicism. All these circumstances combined to spark a deepening in the faith.

When he returned home, he entered college, studying economics and commerce, but an awareness of a call to something more was gradually building. Stephen felt a tension between the way he was living and the way God wanted him to live. Still, he couldn't turn his life around on his own; he desperately needed God's grace. Finally, he summoned the nerve to go to confession after being away from the sacrament for years. The priest who heard his confession was very kind and patient, and gave Stephen some sound advice. At the end of that confession, Stephen revealed the restlessness he felt in his soul. He told the priest – the first time he had told anyone – that he was thinking about the priesthood.

From there, the years flowed by quickly. Stephen went on a retreat, entered the seminary, and in 2000 was ordained a priest. As is the case for so many seminarians, John Paul II became a source of inspiration and a model of sanctity to follow. The Holy Father made his heart burn with the desire to build Christ's kingdom and spread the Gospel.

Just prior to his ordination, Stephen decided to send an invitation to the Holy Father. He didn't expect to get a reply, and he even mentioned that he knew the Pope would be unable to attend. However, in this small way he wanted to tell John Paul II how deeply indebted he was to him, how deeply the Pope's teaching and example had influenced his years of preparation for the priesthood.

Quite to his surprise, he did receive a reply.

"Pope John Paul made an extraordinary gesture of kindness," recounts Father Stephen Savel. "A priest from my diocese was studying in Rome at the time, and one day he was called to the papal apartment. There he was presented with a chalice and the instruction to bring it back with him to Canada." That gold-colored chalice – simple in style, with the papal insignia on the bottom, and a depiction of the Last

Supper around the neck – was an ordination gift for Father Stephen from the Holy Father. Father Stephen uses that chalice regularly and will forever cherish it in remembrance of the spiritual father he loved so much.

A Sudden Stop

Father Richard Mullins still can point out the exact place where their family car screeched to a halt along US-495, Washington's busy beltway. He was in the eighth grade at the time, riding with his mother.

Earlier that week, a priest spoke to his class about vocations, distributing information about the high school seminary in the diocese. Young Richard was interested; he had been thinking about the priesthood and decided he would like to go to that seminary for high school. Yet, at first he didn't mention anything to his parents about the thought. His father was not Catholic, but his mother, a woman of pious Cuban-American stock, raised him in the faith. So Richard kept his idea about the seminary quiet until he was alone with her.

Shortly thereafter, as the two of them were riding in the car, his mother started talking about what it would be like for him to start high school the next fall, going to the local Catholic high school with his older sister. Richard decided that this was the moment to mention his interest in the priesthood:

"You know, mom, there is this high school seminary, and I would really like to go there. I would like to be a priest..."

That was as far as he got before he lurched forward into the dashboard.

"What!" his mother shouted in surprise as she slammed on the breaks, jerked the wheel to the right, and squealed the car to a stop on the shoulder.

"Priesthood? You don't know what you're asking for!" She continued, "You have no idea what kind of life that is; it's a hard life, a life of suffering. You don't want that life – you want a family and a successful career." End of discussion.

After that incident, Richard set aside the idea of becoming a priest for a while. At his parish there was a priest from the Oblates of St. Francis de Sales, so occasionally he would surreptitiously pick up some information from him about the priesthood. In high school Richard had a Jesuit priest for a guidance counselor that discussed the priesthood with him. However, at home he literally had to keep the vocations material under his mattress. At night, he would take out the newsletters and flyers from different seminaries and read them with a flashlight. He just loved it – stories in the Jesuit magazine with testimonies from the guys who were entering the seminary, pamphlets sent by the Oblates, pictures of the seminarians, etc.

Nevertheless, any time he tried to bring up the topic with his parents, he always met with opposition. Just before his high school graduation, he broached the possibility of going to a college seminary. They objected, "What if you change your mind? What if you get there and decide to leave? You'll be throwing away part of your life; you'll have a useless philosophy degree and end up forced to work at Wal-Mart!"

Yet, through all this, several things helped him to persevere in his resolve to continue on toward the vocation. When he would come back home from college, he would serve Mass at the Basilica of the Immaculate Conception in Washington, D.C. At the basilica there was a great culture of support for priestly vocations, largely fostered by the rector of the basilica at the time, Msgr. Michael J. Bransfield (now bishop of Wheeling-Charleston, West Virginia). Here, Richard met other young men who shared his interest in the priesthood. Out of that group, many others also have responded to the priestly call: one became a Dominican, two ended up entering an Augustinian community in Austria, and another went to the Oratorian Fathers.

This group was an amazing source of encouragement for Richard, "Whenever I would go there, I felt tremendous support. Msgr. Bransfield – a priest with a huge Marian devotion, who talks about the Blessed Mother as though she were either right next to him or in the next room – would always keep asking, 'When are you going to the seminary? When will you start? Don't give up on your vocation; you need to do this.'"

For Richard, this was the first time in his life that someone backed him up about the priesthood, and that gave him courage. Finally, in 1989, the year after graduating from college, while he was working for the Red Cross, Richard decided to take the next step. "In the end," he says, "I got up the nerve and went to Father Gould [the vocation director for the Diocese of Arlington, Virgina] and thought it would be a dramatic moment. On the contrary, he simply brought me to his office and asked a few nonchalant questions: 'What's your spiritual life like, your academic life, your social life… Are there any kids running around with your face on them?' Then in a very straightforward way he said, 'Here's a set of breviaries; now go get your physical and psychological exams, and here's the application for seminary. Get to it, and bring it all back to me.'"

Confrontation

In seminary applications, copies of some standard documents are requested: academic transcripts, baptismal and confirmation certificates, and a parental marriage certificate. Richard, living back at home since college graduation, made the mistake of requesting that these documents be sent to the house. Usually, he would pick up the mail when it arrived, but on the occasion when his parents' marriage certificate showed up, his mother beat him to the mailbox. The return address on the outside of the envelope was a giveaway: Church of the Little Flower, Coral Gables, Florida. Her jaw dropped open in shock, and she tore open the envelope. Only one event in the history of their family had taken place at that church: her wedding day. She pulled out the letter's contents and instantly saw the marriage certificate. A single disturbing thought popped into her mind to explain why her son would need their marriage certificate – he must be eloping. There must be some girl that she would disapprove of, some brazen hussy, and her son was trying run off to get married secretly. What could he be thinking! Did he actually think he could get away with this? How could he!

The moment of confrontation arrived. Waving the incriminating letter in one hand, she banged on Richard's door, demanding that he speak with her that instant. And the showdown began. She was yelling and crying – both very uncharacteristic of his usually even-tempered mother. "Mother, mother, I'm not getting married," he blurted in an attempt to calm her down, "I'm going to the seminary."

Big mistake.

That comment was like throwing gasoline on a raging fire. She exploded into tears.

Admittedly, this was not the way Richard had hoped to break the news to his mother, but nonetheless he was glad. At last everyone was on the same page. After the initial shock of the news wore off, his parents gradually came to accept and even support his vocation. This is so often the case when a young man enters the seminary. Usually it's a sacrifice for his family to let him go, but time and again, the Lord blesses that type of sacrifice. Quite often this sacrifice leads a family to grow together in the faith, elevating the natural love of parent and child to a purer, more spiritual plane.

Father Richard experienced this firsthand. "Eventually, everyone's position totally turned around. First, my parents were opposed, and my grandparents, who lived with us, were disappointed because they wanted me to have a career. They all were on edge when I entered the seminary. But in time they came full circle and heartily supported my vocation. I was already a deacon when my grandmother died, and I was able to accompany her during her last moments – a great blessing. My father passed away in 2000. He was proud to have a son as a priest, considering himself an 'honorary Catholic.' Just a short time before he died, he told me, 'You know, I'm finally going to do this thing. I'm going to convert; I want to be Catholic.'

"My mother also grew in her faith on account of my vocation. On one occasion, I mentioned one of my companions who had abandoned his vocation, and my mother commented, 'That's terrible! I can't believe that anyone would ever want to leave behind the priesthood, that's the best vocation that anyone could ever have.' Hearing that from my mother was the most incredible thing. She went from being initially shocked and upset to having this beautiful, loving acceptance of my vocation."

In a Giant's Footsteps

Father Richard has always felt a great kinship with John Paul II. The fact that the Pope was from a communist country and had experienced religious persecution resonated with his family, especially the Cuban-American side. Here was a Pope who understood human suffering and the evils of the world.

There also was the Fatima link. John Paul was shot on May 13, 1981, on the feast of Our Lady of Fatima, and he always credited his survival to Mary's motherly care: "One hand fired and another guided the bullet."

"Looking at the Holy Father," Father Richard says, "I realized that I really wanted to be like him. I wanted to be part of whatever Our Lady wanted for the church, part of what she was seeking to bring to the world."

Father Richard remembers hearing the reports of the assassination attempt, and later on, the accounts of a link to the third "secret" of Fatima, a vision in which three Portuguese shepherd children beheld "a bishop clothed in white" fall to the ground wounded by gunfire. As time progressed, the meaning of that vision would come more fully to light, especially in the announcement made by Cardinal Angelo Sodano upon the beatification of two of the visionaries (the third visionary, Sister Lucia, lived until 2005):

> *On this solemn occasion of his visit to Fatima, His Holiness has directed me to make an announcement to you…he also wishes his pilgrimage to be a renewed gesture of gratitude to Our Lady for her protection during these years of his papacy. This protection seems also to be linked to the so-called third part of the "secret" of Fatima….*

The vision of Fatima concerns above all the war waged by atheistic systems against the Church and Christians, and it describes the immense suffering endured by the witnesses of the faith in the last century of the second millennium. It is an interminable Way of the Cross led by the Popes of the twentieth century.

According to the interpretation of the "little shepherds," which was also confirmed recently by Sister Lucia, "the bishop clothed in white" who prays for all the faithful is the Pope. As he makes his way with great difficulty towards the cross amid the corpses of those who were martyred (bishops, priests, men and women religious, and many lay people), he too falls to the ground, apparently dead, under a hail of gunfire.

After the assassination attempt of 13 May 1981, it appeared evident that it was "a mother's hand that guided the bullet's path," enabling "the Pope in his throes" to halt "at the threshold of death."[16] *On the occasion of a visit to Rome by the then bishop of Leiria-Fatima, the Pope decided to give him the bullet which had remained in the jeep after the assassination attempt, so that it might be kept in the shrine. By the Bishop's decision, the bullet was later set in the crown of the statue of Our Lady of Fatima.*[17]

All the events surrounding the assassination attempt brought back to Father Richard's mind a prayer that he had long ago placed in the hands of Our Lady of Fatima. A traveling statue of her had come to his grade school five years earlier, and in front of the statue, they had a little foil-covered shoebox with a slit in the top for petitions. He had slipped in a note offering his life to Mary: "Blessed Mother, if you want me to be a priest, I'll be a priest."

Through the years, Father Richard increased in his resolve to stand at the Pope's side. Just shortly after Father Richard was ordained, the Holy Father announced his plan to visit Cuba from January 21-26, 1998. The Pope asked priests from around the world to assist with the visit. "Many relatives tried to discourage me," Father Richard recalls. "They said I shouldn't go back there, that there might be problems, that it might be dangerous. But I remember thinking, 'If the Holy Father is going there to win souls, then he is going to need priests, he is going to need me to help him out.' That was a tremendous time of grace, and a chance for me to surrender more to the church and the Holy Father's desires, rather than capitulating to my personal fears."

An Evening at the Concert

Like many other fortunate priests, Father Richard treasures memories of his personal encounters with John Paul. On the first occasion, he was still a seminarian. Monsignor Bransfield, rector of Immaculate Conception Basilica, invited him to come along to Rome with a group accompanying the Shrine Choir. A wealthy benefactor of the music school at the Catholic University of America, Ben Rome – a Jewish man who also was honored as a papal knight – had arranged for the choir to present a concert for the Pope.

Richard gladly went on the trip, with the hope that he would have the chance to see John Paul II, at least from a distance at a Wednesday audience or the Sunday Angelus in St. Peter's Square. Any opportunity was good enough, even if the Pope was just a pinpoint in a crowd.

But he was in for more than he bargained. When the day of the Pope's choir concert arrived, Monsignor Bransfield told Richard to meet him at his hotel and not to be late. As it turned out, the choir concert for the Pope was very private; basically, the only outside guests were from the university's board of trustees. There was only one way Monsignor Bransfield could get Richard into the concert: sitting in the backseat of the Mercedes limo he had rented for Ben Rome!

So off they went, through the Porta Sant'Anna and into the Vatican in the back of a limo. They passed through the gates, and the Swiss guards saluted. Ben Rome was wearing his big papal medal, with Richard on one side and Monsignor Bransfield up in front. The limo stopped, and they were whooshed up the elevator into the papal palace. Before the concert began, Richard was sitting next to Monsignor Lori, who was then a secretary for Cardinal Hickey but now is bishop of Bridgeport, Connecticut. Monsignor Lori asked Richard, "Have you ever met the Holy Father?" Richard said, "No."

Then Monsignor Lori told him what to do: "When the Holy Father enters the room, step up and stand beside the people in the front row, between them and the doorway." That was exactly what Father Richard did. At first, when the

Holy Father came into the room, he went directly toward his chair. Richard thought he had missed his chance, but abruptly the Pope stopped, turned around, and came back to greet everyone in the first row.

"That was the moment I got to shake hands with the Holy Father," Father Richard says, "and he looked at me with an intense look. When he looked at anyone, you had his rapt attention, it was like he was praying for you, like he was involved in your soul in that moment."

In truth, Father Richard's impression is probably right. John Paul, in his memoir about his years as a bishop, *Rise, Let Us Be on Our Way*, mentions his belief that prayer in a way permitted him to know people whom he would meet only for a brief moment. He writes, "In such meetings, if we are truly open, we can come to know and understand one another, even when there is little time...As soon as I meet people, I pray for them, and this helps me in all my relationships."[18]

Blessing Cup

On another occasion, as a deacon, Father Richard was able to present his mother to the Holy Father after one of the Pope's private morning Masses. He said, "Holy Father, this is my mother." The Pope replied, "Oh! You are a holy family." As the Pope moved on, Father Richard's mother was just crying and crying. Then she looked up and said with a bit of a humorous tone, "Honey, I think we've got him fooled!"

During this trip, because his ordination day was approaching, Richard bought his first chalice, an antique silver one restored by a silversmith in Rome. He had heard that the Pope liked to use the chalices of those who were about to be ordained, so he left the chalice with a fellow seminarian studying in Rome. That friend took the cup to the Bronze Doors where Msgr. Dziwitz signed for it and told him to come back in a month.

Father Richard was delighted: "Pope John Paul the Great used my chalice on March 24, 1994 and his secretary sent a card along to that effect. When the chalice arrived in the U.S., there it was complete with the Holy Father's fingerprints... From the day of my first Mass, I felt a special unity with our Holy Father. We had used the same vessel, 'raising up the cup of salvation and calling on the name of the Lord' to make present the same Blood of Christ. As the Holy Father's health declined and his sufferings increased, the chalice took on new significance: 'Can you drink of the cup from which I am to drink?'"

That brings to Father Richard's mind his final memory of the pontiff. "I was in the audience hall, and some Polish nuns were there, so I asked them how to say a few words in Polish. They taught me a couple phrases, but when the Pope came around I was nervous, and rather than saying, 'How are you?' I said. 'How's your health?' The Holy Father looked at me, put his fist to his heart, and pounded it a couple times, saying with a grin, 'Good, good.' That was in 2004, and it was the last time I saw him. But it shows vividly how even in his sickness, even in his infirmity, he was a witness to the dignity of suffering and the dignity of aging, the sanctity of human life at all of its stages. John Paul II touched millions upon millions of people, and he reinvigorated our generation. He reinvigorated the church and the youth. He taught us to set the world ablaze."

Father Álvaro Corcuera *is general director of the religious congregation, the Legionaries of Christ.*

Father Stephen Savel *is a priest in the diocese of London, Ontario. He currently serves as pastor of St. Phillip's parish in Petrolia and Holy Rosary parish in Wyoming, Ontario.*

Father Richard A. Mullins *is director of multicultural ministries for the diocese of Arlington, Virginia.*

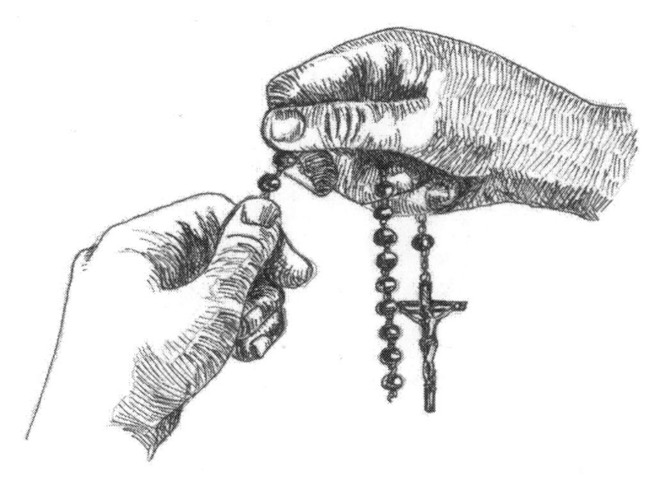

Chapter 3
THE ROSARY

Beads on a String

Anyone who wanders into St. Mary of the Assumption Church in Upper Marlboro, Maryland, at just the right moment during the Easter season, might catch a glimpse of Father Mark praying the Rosary, with a delicate string of white beads dangling from his hand, like points of light standing out against the background of his black cassock. Of course, nothing is uncommon about finding a priest praying the Rosary at his parish church. However, in the case of Father Mark White, there is more to the story. For him, those rosary beads have a very special meaning. They are a reminder that his own spiritual life is forever intertwined with the life of John Paul II.

The Holy Father once reflected about the levels of symbolism that can be seen in a simple string of rosary beads:

> *At the most superficial level, the beads often become a simple counting mechanism…Yet they can also take on a symbolism which can give added depth to contemplation. Here the first thing to note is the way the beads converge upon the crucifix, which both opens and closes the unfolding sequence of prayer. The life and prayer of believers is centered upon Christ. Everything begins from him, everything leads towards him, everything, through him, in the Holy Spirit, attains to the Father.*
>
> *As a counting mechanism, marking the progress of the prayer, the beads evoke the unending path of contemplation and of Christian perfection… A fine way to expand the symbolism of the beads is to let them remind us of our many relationships, of the bond of communion and fraternity which unites us all in Christ.*[19]

For Father Mark, these words of the Holy Father are particularly apt, for the events of his own life, one after another, converged upon Christ's mysterious plan. In the Rosary, Father Mark is reminded of how his special relationship with the Holy Father developed.

Mysterious Calling

Father Mark is a vibrant, profoundly spiritual priest, ordained in 2003. Many of the children at the parish school, who look forward to Father Mark's weekly religion classes, would never guess that Father Mark wasn't always Catholic. The truth is that he grew up as a Lutheran, and at one point he was thinking about becoming a Lutheran minister. However, all that would change in a single, grace-filled instant spent in the Eucharistic presence of Christ.

The event happened in 1991, while he was attending Williams College in Williamstown, Massachusetts. For the first time in his life he had the chance to go into a Catholic church, and something mysteriously inexplicable happened.

"I was immediately aware that I was in the presence of God," Father Mark says, "in a way that I never had been before, and that was really the turning point of my whole life."

After that surprising spiritual experience, he was aware that God had some plan for his life, and that all God was asking him to do was to obey. "Shortly afterwards," he says, "I got this picture in my mind of myself in a cassock as a Catholic priest that was just crystal clear, and I knew that was God's plan for me."

With little hesitation, Father Mark heeded the Lord's prompting and started the process of preparation in order to become Catholic. On Holy Saturday of 1992, he joyfully received the sacraments of confirmation and the Eucharist, becoming a full member of the Catholic Church.

At first, his parents were happy to see Father Mark come into the church because they could tell that it was due to a deep religious commitment, and they were glad for him. His brother was a little more suspicious of the whole thing. However, when he told his family that he wanted to be a priest, that announcement was a bit harder to handle. "They did not immediately go for that," he says, "especially my mom, for whom it took a long time."

Yet as the years went by, both his parents came around to the idea. His father, who passed away a few years ago, in the end was extremely happy for him. Before his death, Father Mark had the joy to receive him into the church and give him the sacraments. "My mom remains Protestant, but she really loves being the mother of a priest. She appreciates that I am doing the Lord's work, and she is very happy to have a son as a priest."

Remarkably, through this entire process, even prior to his conversion, Father Mark already had a deep admiration for John Paul II. "I knew that he was speaking the truth in the world in a way that nobody else really was," he says. After he entered the church, he learned a huge amount from the writings that the Holy Father personally penned and from the other documents he promulgated, especially the Catechism of the Catholic Church.

When Father Mark finished college, a priest advised him to allow a little more time to pass before entering the seminary. So, in the meantime, Father Mark taught middle school for a couple of years. When he finally commenced theology studies at the Catholic University of America, John Paul's writing remained a constant companion throughout.

"We had a group there in the seminary that was very devoted to John Paul II," he remembers. "We would get together and read his encyclicals and discuss them." During Father Mark's second year of theology, this group organized a trip to Rome during spring break, in the Great Jubilee Year of 2000. Their group was privileged to get on the list to attend the Pope's morning Mass.

"It was the day after Ash Wednesday of the year 2000," Father Mark says. "We got to go to his private chapel where we had Mass with him and met with him afterwards."

To be able to meet the Pope and receive his encouragement was a special blessing.

"I'll never forget that day and that moment," he says. "It was before September 11, and there wasn't much security. I was actually amazed at how little security there was. They led us through the various hallways in the apostolic palace, and before we knew it we were going through a door, turning a corner, and there was the chapel, and there the Pope was on his knees in front of the altar, totally consumed in prayer – completely consumed with intense prayer. So we quietly entered the chapel and took our places. To see his devotion in saying Mass, and the beauty of his priesthood, to see the total faith that he had in everything that he did was a great gift."

After the ceremony ended, the Holy Father greeted the handful of guests that were present, going from person to person, as each responded with reverence and kissed his ring.

"When the Pope addressed our group," Father Mark recalls, "he said, 'America, the future is bright!'"

When the Holy Father reached Father Mark, they grasped hands, and the Pontiff pressed a rosary into his palm. Father Mark cherishes that rosary as a memento of his love for the Holy Father. He likes to use it during the Easter season because its beads are white, but for the rest of the year he keeps it safely tucked away because he doesn't want to wear it out.

At the School of Mary

Needless to say, Father Mark did not own a rosary as a child. Growing up as a Protestant, he was fortunate to develop a deep relationship of prayer with Jesus, with whom he would talk as a friend. However, a relationship with Jesus' mother, Mary, was something that he lacked. His Protestant pastors were opposed to the idea that Mary deserved special treatment, and he never had any role models to demonstrate an authentic love for the Mother of God. Devotion to the Blessed Virgin Mary was something he learned only later from John Paul II's witness.

After becoming Catholic, Father Mark grew in his appreciation for Mary by reading what the Holy Father had written on the topic and by imitating his example. For instance, John Paul II's motto, *Totus Tuus*, is a reference to St. Louis de Montfort's prayer of total consecration to Mary, whereby the Holy Father had entrusted himself to the care of the Blessed

Virgin. Father Mark has imitated John Paul II by making that same consecration and trying to practice it like he did.

"The Holy Father has helped me enormously to trust our Lady and to know that she is watching over me," he says.

But being a loyal son of Mary entails many points. Foremost, it entails holding the mystery of the faith firmly, and being a public witness of that mystery – an aspect very central to Father Mark's vision of the priesthood. He always admired how courageously John Paul II witnessed to the fact that Jesus Christ is the Son of God and demonstrated that the truth is absolutely worth giving your life for. Everything the Pope did, even down to the details of how he stood and spoke communicated that truth.

"I am not anywhere near the man he is," says Father Mark, "but I try to imitate him. I try to show in everything I say and do that I believe our Catholic faith with everything I have, and that I would give my life for it with the help of God's grace."

He also tries to imitate the great fatherly love with which John Paul invited everyone to come to God's mercy. "Again, I can't rival the fatherly love that he had, but I try to foster it as best I can," Father Mark says.

With that in mind, he makes a point of visiting the grade school religion classes each week. The kids all know him and look forward to his classes, which are rumored to be a lot of fun!

"Practically every day there is a moment when I can see God's grace working through me as an instrument," he says. "Some of my best memories are of seeing the faith of the children at the parish school come alive, seeing them grow in love for Christ, Mary, and the saints. To see the way God is working in their lives is remarkable and humbling. I am humbled to realize that this work surpasses me and to see God working through me."

Like John Paul II, Father Mark finds enduring optimism when he considers the Church's young people. They offer hope for a new future, the hope that tomorrow will be a little brighter than today. He humbly offers himself as a spiritual father, entrusting them all to Jesus through Mary.

Omnes ad Iesum per Mariam.

Motherly Touch

If you ever travel through the town of Peekskill, New York, on the eastern shore of the Hudson, don't miss the opportunity to stop by Assumption Church. The church's unconventional design has a long history. Originally, the building was designed as a theater, with a raised stage and balcony seating running along three of the walls. The small parish church was across the street, but in the 1920s, the local Catholic population started to grow rapidly, and the theater was converted into a place of worship – the old church became the rectory.

Yet perhaps the building's unusual history is precisely what accounts for its unique charm. The vintage elegance of a classic turn-of-the-century theater blends with beautiful devotional artwork and tasteful decor. Quite conspicuous are seven large stained glass windows down the walls on each side of the church, near the ceiling, each portraying the Blessed Virgin Mary according to the different titles given her in the Litany of Loreto – Mystical Rose, Tower of Ivory, Ark of the Covenant, Queen of Angels, and others.

Father John Higgins explained the symbolism behind each depiction when I had the chance to visit his parish back in 2007, coincidentally on the eleventh anniversary of his priestly ordination. Father John is a serene and courteous priest, thoughtful in speech and gentlemanly in manner. At first, it is easy not to pick up on the intensity of his character. He pours himself completely into any task he undertakes.

Back in high school, he was passionately competitive, especially in golf. After graduation, he even had the chance to go professional, but he decided to leave it all behind to join the priesthood. When he was ordained, his hometown golf course honored him with a courtesy membership.

So, don't be fooled. Beneath Father John's mild-mannered exterior still beats the fiery heart of an aggressive competitor, the heart of a zealous apostle.

Father John is currently head pastor at Assumption Church. (The name "Assumption" references the occasion when the Blessed Virgin Mary was taken body and soul into heaven.) Previously, his first parish assignment had been as assistant pastor for six years at Holy Rosary Church in the Bronx. Perhaps the Blessed Mother is trying to convey a subtle – or not so subtle – message: she remains at his side.

Father John is definitely someone who vouches for the special care Mary takes of those her Son calls to the priesthood. He has experienced this reality firsthand, initially as a seminarian, and later as a priest. "As for proof," he says, "there are millions of points of proof. Mary is the mother of Christ, and if a priest is 'another Christ,' then she is the mother of priests in a special manner. She shows her motherly care in a myriad of ways. I have certainly experienced this as a priest in the countless favors she has done for me. I am sure that she treats other priests and seminarians with equal love and affection. But as for those who have a special devotion to her, I think she rewards them in full measure and overflowing."

John Paul II would have agreed.

Jesus gives his Mother to you so that she will comfort you with her tenderness… She will discharge her ministry as a mother and train you and mold you until Christ is fully formed in you.[20] *This is why I now wish to repeat the motto of my episcopal and pontifical service:* "Totus tuus." *Throughout my life I have experienced the loving and forceful presence of the Mother of Our Lord. Mary accompanies me every day in the fulfillment of my mission as successor of Peter. Mary is the Mother of divine grace, because she is the Mother of the Author of grace. Entrust yourselves to her with complete confidence!*[21]

A Gift from Mom

On Saturday, October 7, 1995, the feast of the Our Lady of the Rosary, Father John believes it was the Blessed Mother who gave him a special gift. One week earlier, he had been ordained to the diaconate at St. Joseph Seminary in New York, where he was still finishing his fourth year of theology. That Friday, John Paul II came to visit St. Joseph Seminary and prayed vespers in the main chapel together with all the professors and students there. He had some challenging words for the seminarians, reminding them to take courage in face of their vocation and to turn to the Blessed Mother whenever their nerve began to waiver.

If you are to become priests, it will be for the purpose – above all other purposes – of proclaiming the Word of God and feeding God's people with the Body and Blood of Christ…. Over the magnificent doors of this chapel I am able to read words that have a very special meaning for me: "Aperite portas Redemptori." *These were my words to the peoples of the world at the very beginning of my pontificate: "Help the Pope," I said, "and all those who wish to serve Christ and with Christ's*

> *power to serve the human person and the whole of mankind. Do not be afraid! Open wide the doors for Christ"!*[22]
>
> *Do not be afraid, I say, because great courage is required if we are to open the doors to Christ, if we are to let Christ enter into our hearts... Open the doors of your hearts in order that Christ may enter and bring you his joy. The Church needs joyful priests, capable of bringing true joy to God's people, which is the Good News in all its truth and transforming power... Above all, I encourage you, the seminarians, to be unselfish in answering the call of Christ and in offering your lives to his church. Do not be afraid! If you begin to lose courage, turn to Mary, Seat of Wisdom; with her at your side, you will never be afraid.*[23]

Father John was there in the seminary chapel as the Holy Father entered. "I remember being overwhelmed by his oncoming presence," he says. "As he came down the aisle and I greeted him, I remember looking into his eyes, and in that moment it seemed as though his face filled the whole universe. For that moment, I felt as though I was the only person in the world, and tears came, and I just turned around and went back to my place. I felt so moved, as though, looking into his face, I saw God.

"The following day was my one week anniversary of being a deacon, and that was when I was chosen to serve as a deacon for the Holy Father at the Mass in Central Park. A vast crowd was gathered there, but despite such high security and so many dignitaries, he still briefly greeted the liturgical ministers ahead of time. It was just a brief meeting where we shook his hand. The occasion was more so an experience of serving with him as he offered the Mass and standing by his side as he did so. I had only been a deacon for six days, and I had the chance not just to be with the Pope at the altar, but even at the sign of peace to embrace him. That was a great honor.

"The Holy Father was beginning to experience the feebleness of age, but still he had a remarkable rapport with young people. Those kids that were present will never forget how in the middle of his homily he broke into song to sing an old Christmas carol that he had learned as a child in Poland."

> *I remember a song I used to sing in Poland as a young man, a song which I still sing as Pope, which tells about the birth of the Savior. On Christmas night, in every church and chapel, this song would ring out, repeating in a musical way the story told in the Gospel. It says: "In the silence of the night, a voice is heard: 'Get up, shepherds, God is born for you! Hurry to Bethlehem to meet the Lord.'" The same story is told in the beautiful hymn, "Silent Night," which everyone knows. That is a hymn which moves us deeply by reminding us that Jesus, the Son of God, was born of Mary, born to make us holy and to make us adopted sons and daughters of God. It is a hymn to the creative power of the Holy Spirit. It is a song to help us not to be afraid.*[24]

Unfortunately, the official text fails to capture the Pope's ad-libbed comments and his spontaneous singing in Polish. However, Father John remembers: "It was so touching, and even when I watch the video, it still causes me to well up with emotion. He was an avuncular figure, like your grandfather singing songs around the kitchen table when you go to visit him. Afterward, the choir chimed in with "Silent Night" in reply at the end of the Pope's homily. No one was expecting it. All of New York was captivated by him."

The Holy Father concluded with a word of encouragement and advice for young people:

> *You young people will live most of your lives in the next millennium. You must help the Holy Spirit to shape its social, moral, and spiritual character. You must transmit your joy in being adopted sons and daughters of God through the creative power of the Holy Spirit. Do this with the help of Mary, Mother of Jesus. Cling to her Rosary, and you will never wander far from her side.* [25]

John Paul II had a deep love for the Blessed Virgin Mary. He was a man who endured countless hardships. He lost his own mother, Emilia, before he was nine. Three years later, his older brother Edmund, already a doctor, died of scarlet fever contracted from a patient. When he was nineteen, Germany invaded Poland, and amid the horrors of the Nazi occupation, his own father died in February of 1941. Young Karol found himself alone in a harsh world. Yet he never gave into bitterness or despair. On the contrary, he turned more deeply to prayer, pouring out the pain and sorrows that lacerated his heart. He still had Christ as his brother, Mary for his mother, and the paternal care of a Heavenly Father. No person or circumstance could deprive him of that.

John Paul's love for Mary never conflicted with his love for Christ. In fact, he considered such a suggestion to be impossible. No one can love Mary to the exclusion of her Son because Mary always leads a devout soul to a more intimate relationship with her Son. Veneration for Mary honors her Son, for it is precisely on account of her role a Mother of the Redeemer that she is revered. Every good son delights to see his mother praised.

In the case of John Paul II, it was his tender relationship with Mary that provided a maternal influence. Mary was the one who smoothed off his rough edges, who bound up his wounded heart, who stood with him at the foot of the cross and taught him to repay hatred with love.

Father John comments, "It seems to me that the heart of his devotion to the Blessed Virgin Mary is something that we will never fully comprehend. One can get a glimpse of it through his prayers and through his writings. The closest I ever came to understanding his love for her was when I once heard him begin to pray to Mary in the middle of a homily. It was profoundly moving; he seemed on the verge of tears as he repeated tenderly, 'O Mary, O, Mary.' Obviously the

Pope's example elicits a response. If this holy man had such an intimate relationship with the Mother of our Savior, then we all ought to cultivate this treasure in our own spiritual lives – so much the more for us priests. It was as a priestly son of Mary that John Paul invoked her name and spoke to her from his heart."

FATHER MARK WHITE *was ordained in 2003 for the Archdiocese of Washington, D.C., where he currently serves.*

FATHER JOHN HIGGINS *is a priest in the Archdiocese of New York. He was ordained on May 11, 1996.*

Chapter 4
ZUCCHETTOS

Questions for the Bishop

Spring's cool breeze gently wafted through the windows of the grade school classroom where I sat with a group of students circled around our graying bishop. As the bishop spoke, many of us had the same question in mind, but no one dared to speak it. After all, he was the bishop, and perhaps some questions were better left unspoken. Nonetheless, one of the sixth graders mustered enough confidence to raise his hand and daringly ask, "Why do you wear a beanie, bishop?"

There was a brief pause.

Then, with a patient grandfatherly tone, our kindly bishop, the Most Reverend Michael McAuliffe, explained to us that his hat was neither a beanie nor a yarmulke. Instead, his cap was properly called a zucchetto. Bishops, cardinals, and popes all wear an appropriately colored zucchetto as a sign of their church office.

The word *zucchetto* originally comes from an Italian word for gourd – thus the resemblance between the words zucchetto and zucchini. The word may have been adopted for clerical skullcaps because they vaguely look like the rounded bottom of a dried gourd. On the other hand, it might have been because what a zucchetto is often used to cover, namely a balding prelate's shining head, has a somewhat gourdish resemblance. In either case, zucchettos remain among the most recognizable pieces of ecclesiastical apparel.

Close Encounter

On September 17, 2003, Brother Juan Carlos Vázquez could almost have leaned out over the guardrail and plucked the zucchetto off of John Paul II's head. That is, of course, if he were a bit taller, and if the Pope were not flanked by undercover Swiss guards commissioned precisely to prevent such an incident. As the Holy Father passed by, Brother Juan, his parents (Carlos and María), his two sisters, and his younger brother were ecstatic. They had been waiting for hours, hoping and praying for just such a papal close encounter.

Their family had come to Rome for the religious profession of some of Brother Juan's seminary companions. Religious profession is the occasion when members of Brother

Juan's religious congregation, the Legion of Christ, first take the vows of poverty, chastity, and obedience. Religious profession is preceded by two years of novitiate, a period dedicated to developing an interior life of prayer and to discerning one's vocation. As is customary in many religious orders, "brother" is the title used to address both novices and professed religious during the years leading up to priestly ordination. Thereafter, the usual title is "father."

A Man of God

Witnessing Brother Juan's companions consecrating their lives to God was a moving experience, but the occasion offered Brother Juan's family another opportunity, which they eagerly seized. While they were in Rome, they would take advantage of the chance to see John Paul II.

Of course, it is one thing to see the Pope, and quite another to see him *up close*. Pilgrims familiar with Rome know that a crowd starts to gather in St. Peter's Square hours before the Wednesday audience begins. To get a good seat, there is only one reliable plan, simple and sure: to be close to the Pope, get there first! If one descends on St. Peter's square early enough, none but a few pigeons and some early-rising nuns will obstruct the most strategic seat.

However, Brother Juan's family had not thought out much of a strategy, although they knew that they needed to arrive in St. Peter's Square well before the start of the audience. Brother Juan, staying with his confreres at the seminary, rose at the crack of dawn so that he could finish his morning prayers before the rendezvous with his family. In fact, they struck out for the papal audience so early that Brother Juan missed breakfast. Still, by the time they arrived at the square, the best areas were already full, and the guards sent them to another section distant from where the Pope would deliver his address.

Sitting there in the square, waiting for hours, Brother Juan's stomach began grumbling. His father noticed something was wrong and asked if he had eaten. "My dad gave me some cheese crackers to eat for breakfast," Brother Juan recalls. The unusual breakfast was memorable as he waited to see the Pope on that sunny September morning.

At last they heard the sound of applause and cheering, first near the back of the square and then following the Pope in a wave as his open-roofed car slowly moved through the crowd. Because they were a long way from the front and several sections to the left of the center aisle, Brother Juan's family expected to content themselves with seeing the Pope from a distance. However, despite their expectations, the Pope's car made a sudden left and passed right in front of their crowed section.

As a young seminarian preparing for the priesthood, the encounter was a tremendous experience for Brother Juan. John Paul II represented all that he was striving toward, the perfect example of a priest living his vocation to the full. Physically, the now-aged John Paul II lacked the physique and vigor of his earlier days. He was no longer the robust, athletic figure that first charmed the world. But his declining outward appearance could not conceal his inner spiritual vibrancy, and it never distanced the Holy Father from the crowds who came to see him. If anything it increased their reverence and awe. In his final years, John Paul II gave living witness to the Gospel mandate to take up the cross, preaching this message with a language more eloquent than words. "When I saw him," notes Brother Juan, "I knew that I was looking at a man of God."

Needless to say, the actual moment of the Pope's approach was intensely emotional. One of Brother Juan's sisters reached for her camera to take a quick snapshot, but after checking her bag and her pockets she realized that it was missing. She had accidentally forgotten it at the hotel that morning. The family left St. Peter's square with great joy, but Brother Juan's sister had a tinge of disappointment about not getting a picture.

However, that disappointment would eventually be remedied. Adjacent to the square, photos from the audiences are always made available by *L'Osservatore Romano,* the Vatican's semiofficial paper. A few months later, one of Brother Juan's fellow seminarians was glancing through the photos there and recognized a familiar face. Sure enough, there was a shot of the Vazquez family standing with arms outstretched in greeting while the Pope passed a few feet away. That providential discovery was like the icing on the cake. "This is just one of the countless small ways that God has shown his loving care for my family," says Brother Juan. That picture is a gift from the Lord that he has not forgotten.

Childhood Confessions

Brother Juan is a lively, almost hyperactive native of Madrid, Spain, who openly confesses to being a rather rambunctious kid. He can remember one occasion when his mother cried because she thought he and his older brother would never learn to get along peacefully. They loved each other, but it was with a characteristically rough-and-tumble brotherly love.

"One time I broke my brother's teeth," Brother Juan admits, "but we have gotten along much better since I entered the seminary."

As kids, the two boys used to share a room and had been roughhousing when the incident occurred. Brother Juan had entered the room and observed his big brother lying heedlessly sprawled out on the floor. He decided to capitalize on the situation by tackling him. A few moments and a couple of cracked teeth later, his mother heard the clamor and came running into the room. Both brothers were pointing to each other and shouting, "He hit me first!"

A Chip Off the Block

Certainly, Brother Juan gets part of his energetic nature from his dad. Brother Juan describes his father, Carlos Vázquez, as a generous, sacrificial man with a deeply spiritual side, a big heart, and a weakness for taking on charitable work. He is passionate about building up the church and working for people in spiritual and physical need.

Carlos is a talented individual; he has studied business and is presently finishing a PhD in psychology. Yet he has always devoted his time to good causes, even though they didn't pay very well. He drew a modest salary as the director of Recal, a non-profit foundation devoted to helping the needy, and he was able to do part-time volunteer work on the side. His wife María also earned some income as a secretary for a Catholic organization. They managed to make ends meet, and that was good enough.

The charitable project closest to Carlos' heart was (and still remains) *Misioneros urbanos de Jesucristo* – translated as the Urban Missionaries of Jesus Christ. This group is dedicated to renewing the faith of the inner city through evangelization, humanitarian efforts, drug rehabilitation, helping the homeless, and aiding the unemployed. Their mission is to bring the light of Christ to poor souls overwhelmed by misfortune in today's society. *Misioneros urbanos* tries to help those who are disadvantaged, and when those people are back on their feet, they often remain in contact for many years. Some choose to become volunteers and in turn help carry on the good work.

In his effort to keep developing the project, Carlos was really exhausting himself in service.

Unexpected Illness

But then the pain in his stomach began. At first it was just when he ate certain foods, but eventually the pain became more persistent, accompanied by serious difficulties with digestion. Soon Carlos was unable to eat solid foods, and his doctor diagnosed him with Crohn's disease.

The causes of Crohn's disease are poorly understood; however, its symptoms are easily recognizable. It afflicts the digestive tract by causing bowel wall inflammation. No cure is known, but a typical mode of treatment entails a restrictive, liquid diet composed of simple sugars and amino acids that pose less digestive difficulty than solid foods.

Later on, at times the pain would make even the liquid diet impossible, and he would have to resort to intravenous fluids. However, in the beginning the liquid diet was exactly what Carlos' doctor advised. Unfortunately, this special liquid regimen is very expensive, around a thousand euros per month. That was much more than Carlos and María could afford. Thus far, the two had been content to live on a small income, willingly sacrificing life's luxuries in order to serve the church. Yet, despite their frugality, they could not cover such a costly medical expense on so modest an income.

Still, at this stage, Carlos was unwilling to abandon his charitable work in order to seek a better paying job. The development of *Misioneros urbanos* had reached a crucial point as Carlos sought official approval for its statutes. He could not believe that God wanted him to cast aside this work in order to seek more lucrative employment. Even if it required great personal sacrifice, even if it posed a risk to his health, Carlos would continue the Lord's work. In any case, before long his poor health would have prevented him from gaining other employment anyway.

There were few options open. The full liquid diet was too expensive, so Carlos simply had to use less of it. Not surprisingly, he gradually began losing weight; his body was literally starving. By September of 2006, his weight had dropped as low as eighty-four pounds. The situation was becoming desperate, so something had to be done.

Initially, Carlos had been diagnosed in a private hospital, but they later sent him away because he was too costly for them. Now his only hope was the public hospital, so he went there to see if he could qualify for a government subsidy under the social health care system in Spain. But his application process ran into a snag. In Spain there is a distinction between privately practicing physicians and those working for the public health care system. All these months Carlos had been seeing a private doctor. However, to apply for social medical aid, it was necessary that his medical records be in the public system from the start. Bureaucracy prevailed and Carlos, though practically skin and bones, was sent away without aid.

By this time, the situation was very serious. He could not keep losing weight much longer, and he could not continue subsisting on such a small amount of nourishment. Carlos and María kept praying for a solution.

Then one day, Carlos woke up with a mysterious inspiration. He felt that he should return to the social health care office and seek aid *immediately*. The idea did not seem very logical. He had already tried applying for aid several times, and everyone assured him that no progress could be made in his case. Without the required records, the processing of his claim was simply impossible. Nonetheless, on this morning he hastened to the office, confident that something would be different.

At the office, Carlos again sought help. His slender appearance alone revealed his plea as no scam, but still his request was denied. However, this time, encouraged by his inspiration, Carlos was not so easily dissuaded. After much arguing and a sequence of chaotic occurrences simultaneously unfolding in the office, the confused secretary agreed to send on his paperwork without the required documents – assuring him that nothing would come of it. Fortunately, she was wrong. Her action set in motion a chain of events leading to Carlos being granted the long sought medical assistance.

Carlos had been given a bit of a reprieve. At least he had enough food to survive on, and his weight loss halted. Nonetheless, he remained very weak, and he still was unable to eat normal food. There seemed to be no hope of an improvement or cure for his condition.

The Relic

Understandably, María remained very worried about the whole situation. During this entire period, she had been constantly asking friends and coworkers to pray for Carlos. Everyone assured her that they would.

One of María's coworkers, a lay consecrated woman in the Regnum Christi movement, had an interesting idea. Some years earlier, an affluent husband and wife in Madrid had provided generous support for a project in the Vatican, a project in which the Holy Father had personal interest. Before John Paul II died, as a sign of gratitude, he sent one of his white papal zucchettos to the couple as a gift. María's coworker knew this couple personally, explained Carlos' illness to them, and asked them to lend the zucchetto to Carlos and María.

Thus, John Paul II's white papal zucchetto came to abide in the Vázquez home, and they began dedicating a special moment of prayer each day to asking for John Paul's intercession. Every day they would come into the living room to pray, using a simple prayer like the following:

O Blessed Trinity
We thank you for having graced the church
with Pope John Paul II
and for allowing the tenderness of your Fatherly care,
the glory of the cross of Christ,
and the splendor of the Holy Spirit,
to shine through him.
Trusting fully in your infinite mercy
and in the maternal intercession of Mary,
he has given us a living image of Jesus the Good Shepherd,

and has shown us that holiness
is the necessary measure of ordinary Christian life
and is the way of achieving eternal communion with you.
Grant us, by his intercession, and according to your will,

[here Carlos and María would add, *"for the sake of the salvation of souls"]*

the graces we implore,
hoping that he will soon be numbered
among your saints. Amen. [26]

Carlos says that he never prayed for a cure, only that he would be granted the strength to continue doing his work for the church. However, others were bolder – his wife, children, cousins, family, the Regnum Christi consecrated women, and friends all were praying for a cure.

The whole situation revealed their great faith and was reminiscent of Biblical accounts. After all, in the Gospel a woman was once healed by merely touching Christ's cloak. Also, in the Acts of the Apostles it is recounted that the deeds accomplished at the hands of Paul were so extraordinary "…that when facecloths or aprons that touched his skin were applied to the sick, their diseases left them and the evil spirits came out of them."[27]

If God worked such wonders through St. Paul, perhaps he would permit a something similar to happen for the honor of John Paul II.

Dreams

Nonetheless, as the days passed, Carlos' condition did not improve. On November 14, 2006, he went to bed as normal, weak, still with the pain, and still unable to eat. But that night was destined to be a turning point.

In the early hours of the morning, Carlos had a dream. He is unwilling to speak about all the details, but in the dream he saw John Paul II, who told Carlos to eat whatever he wanted because he needed strength to help save many souls. Carlos awoke with a start, and immediately noticed a strange difference.

He didn't feel any pain.

Previously, he had not been without pain – even on the occasions when doctors had administered morphine. But now he felt so good that he decided to go down to the kitchen to do some cleaning. When his wife awoke, she was surprised to find Carlos scrubbing pots and pans. This was something she had not seen in months. Carlos felt so well that he was inclined to try and eat something. He called his doctor to ask for an opinion, but the doctor's response was vehemently negative. The doctor said that under no circumstance should he eat solid food – it didn't matter how much better he felt; it was impossible for his disease to have simply vanished. His condition could not have gotten better overnight.

But he did not care about the doctor's skeptical response. He still did not feel any pain. That day, a couple of his uncles were in town, and they invited Carlos to join them for a drive.

As the hours passed and Carlos saw that the pain did not return, he decided to disclose that he thought he was cured.

When he told them that the pain had left, their first reaction was to shout, "It's a miracle! It's a miracle! Let's go eat!"

So they stopped the car at a restaurant. In front of his amazed uncles, he signaled for the waiter and ordered a big, juicy steak, a double espresso coffee, and Spanish liquor. When the food arrived and he started eating, his uncles were still astounded. How could this be? For Carlos, a few bites of this type of food should have serious consequences – a meal like this could have killed him.

At his uncles' prompting, Carlos explained the events of the previous days, including the prayer and his dream about John Paul II. They were overjoyed. "It's a miracle; it's a miracle!" One of his uncles started calling relatives on his cell phone. Carlos called María while she was driving home; she was overcome with joy at the news. Carlos was cured. A chaotic and exuberant celebration ensued: rejoicing, shouting, and crying in that little restaurant in Madrid on the evening of November 15, 2006.

The Real Miracle

Was Carlos' cure a miracle? I cannot say for sure; such matters are for the church to decide, though I can attest that when I last saw Carlos, he had gained weight and looked remarkably better. However, this much is sure, the Vázquez family is itself a living miracle. In the midst of a secularized

Spain, all five of their children want to dedicate their lives to the Lord's service. The three boys, Brother José, Brother Juan, and Brother Santiago are Legionaries of Christ and on the path to the priesthood. Both of their sisters are lay consecrated members of the Regnum Christi movement.

So what effect have these remarkable events had on Brother Juan? John Paul II has left his special mark this young seminarian's heart. John Paul II is not just a role model, an example of a holy priest, and a beloved pontiff, but also someone who still watches over his family with fatherly care. This special relationship with John Paul II will continue to have a great effect on Brother Juan throughout his remaining time of preparation for the priesthood and will assuredly influence the type of priest he becomes.

Brother Juan Carlos Vázquez *is a seminarian with the Legionaries of Christ.*

Chapter 5
THE POPE'S CANOE

Summer's End at Orchard Lake

The hot afternoon sun shimmered on the glassy surface of Orchard Lake, playing here and there with the waves of a passing duck or dancing across the concentric splash of a restless perch. On a day like today, when the still air hung heavy and humid, the cool waters looked inviting. As he walked by, Cardinal Karol Wojtyla cast a wistful glance toward the large island in the center, a half-mile from the doughnut-shaped lake's shore, and sighed.

It all started when Father Walter J. Ziemba was appointed head of the Orchard Lake Schools, comprised of SS. Cyril and Methodius Seminary, St. Mary's College, and St. Mary's

Preparatory. Father Ziemba had many personal ties to Poland and a keen interest in facilitating dialogue between Polish and American churchmen. Soon after his appointment, he invited Cardinal Stefan Wyszynski, the primate of Poland, to visit the Orchard Lake Schools.

Orchard Lake is located beyond the outskirts of Detroit, Michigan, northwest of the city, in the heart of the Great Lakes Region – once a thriving center for heavy industry, attracting scores of Polish immigrants. St. Mary's College, with its department of Polish Language and Letters, helped to preserve a rich cultural heritage. Cardinal Wyszynski would gladly have accepted Father Ziemba's invitation, but there was one problem. The embattled cardinal feared the communist authorities would hinder his return to Poland if he left the country. Consequently, he suggested that Poland's other red biretta, Cardinal Karol Wojtyla, be invited in his place.

Cardinal Wojtyla ultimately accepted invitations to Orchard Lake on two occasions: in 1969 and 1976. Msgr. Frank Koper was a young member of the seminary faculty during the 1976 visit, and he remembers it well. A three-day conference was convened on the topic of "Polonia" – a name for the United State's substantial Polish American community. Cardinal Wojtyla, nineteen other bishops, and the seminary faculty attended the lengthy conference sessions. They shared stories about their experiences with Polonia and considered the struggles Polish immigrants faced to maintain their faith in a hostile environment. The ability of Polish parishes and neighborhoods to offer support and serve as vehicles for fostering integration into American society was noted.

One hot afternoon, as the sessions wore on, Cardinal Wojtyla was exhausted by the discussion and said, "Enough!" He told one of the faculty members that he would like to go canoeing on Orchard Lake. Msgr. Zdzislaw Peszkowski, a professor of Polish Literature at St. Mary's, found a kayak and arranged for it to be brought for the cardinal.

Thus, the cardinal glided gracefully across the mile-wide waters, refreshing his mind and soul. It was a moment of respite amid a life often faced with rough waters.

Of course, the cardinal's outing soon became the talk of campus. The kayak was kept, reputedly surviving to the present in the basement of the Orchard Lake Castle where the college chancellor resides.

Prophecy

As the fall semester of 1977 progressed, Gary Dailey was thrilled about his upcoming pilgrimage to Rome. A wealthy gentleman in his small hometown of Adams, Massachusetts, was paying for groups from the three parishes in the area to attend the celebration of the fortieth anniversary of the priesthood for Cardinal Egidio Vagnozzi, who had served as apostolic delegate to the United States from 1958 to 1968. Gary was just beginning his freshman year at St. Mary's at

Orchard Lake, Michigan. Despite having an Irish-sounding last name – "Dailey" would look at home painted on a Dublin mailbox – his grandparents are from Poland. He chose to attend St. Mary's College so that he could keep the Polish language alive, and now he speaks Polish fluently.

Gary was understandably excited that his hometown pastor invited him on the pilgrimage, and he reacted by sharing the news with all his friends at college. Gary's Polish language professor, Msgr. Zdzislaw Peszkowski, heard the news with interest. The professor, who the previous year had tracked down a kayak for Cardinal Wojtyla, was also a friend of Cardinal Wyszynski and used to serve as the cardinal's confessor whenever he was in Poland.

When Msgr. Peszkowski discovered that Gary was traveling to Rome, he asked him to carry out a special mission. Correspondence sent to recipients in Poland was unreliable and often subject to inspection by the communists. In fact, the bishops of Poland were under frequent surveillance by government authorities. Cardinal Wyszynski suffered thirty-six months of confinement before being released in 1956. Cardinal Wojtyla was aware that his Krakow residence was bugged by the secret police, so he would take dignitaries into the mountains for talks in order to have a little more privacy.[28]

With this in mind, Msgr. Peszkowski, gave Gary two sealed letters with instructions to hand-deliver them to the Polish cardinals: one for Cardinal Wyszynki and another for Cardinal Wojtyla. The two cardinals would be at the Polish college in Rome for an important meeting, which coincidentally coincided with the timing of the festivities honoring Cardinal Vagnozzi. Gary never learned the contents of those letters, but he carried out the task faithfully.

When he arrived in Rome, he made an appointment to meet Cardinal Wyszynski at the Polish College, the national residence for Polish seminarians studying in Rome. "Cardinal Wyszynski was celebrating Mass when I arrived," Father Gary remembers. "But after Mass he met me, and I handed the letter to him personally. He wanted to sign a prayer card for me with the picture of Our Lady of Czestochowa, but we were out in the hallway where there was no table. So the Cardinal asked me to stand still, and he signed the card on my back. I still have that prayer card in my breviary to this day."

Gary mentioned that he also had a letter for Cardinal Wojtyla and asked how to contact him. Cardinal Wyszynski recommended calling Wojtyla's young secretary, Father Stanislaw Dziwisz, who had accompanied him during the trip to Rome.

Gary left a message for Father Dziwisz, who promptly called back. "Cardinal Wojtyla has asked you to come serve Mass for him at St. Peter's Tomb at eight o'clock tomorrow morning," he said, "and you may bring your pastor and another priest if you would like."

Accompanied by his pastor, Father John Chwalek, and the priest who baptized him, Father Eugene Ozimek, Gary waited anxiously in the cavernous sacristy of St. Peter's Basilica at eight o'clock the next morning. Soon he heard the approach of clacking footsteps, and a moment later he saw Cardinal Wojtyla with his secretary close behind. Without introduction, the cardinal walked directly toward Gary, who stood with a conspicuous letter in his hands. Then, after a few words, the cardinal led him over to a vesting table and signaled for him to help with preparations for Mass. Down in the crypt beneath the basilica's floor, at the altar facing the final resting place of St. Peter's bones, Gary served the cardinal's Mass. Only Father Dziwisz and the two priests from Gary's town were present.

"Watching him celebrate Mass at St. Peter's tomb was timeless," says Father Gary. "That moment was like a piece of eternity. Not so much that he was a cardinal, although that was something great – after all how many cardinals do you meet when you're a freshman in college? It wasn't just meeting a cardinal; serving Mass for him was different. It was an experience of his holiness. He celebrated Mass as if no one else were around him. There was such an aura of concentration, and I remember that very vividly."

After the Mass, they all exchanged greetings before parting. Father Gary remembers, as clear as if it were yesterday, walking out the doors of St. Peter's Basilica and saying to his pastor, "Wouldn't it be awesome if he was elected Pope?" That was November of 1977.

In October of 1978, Gary's pastor was again in Rome. He was there below the balcony overlooking St. Peter's square when Cardinal Pericle Felici made the announcement, *"Habemus Papam!"* (We have a Pope!) An instant later, Cardinal Wojtyla stepped into view, henceforth as Pope John Paul II.

"My pastor hastily sent me a telegram at college," Father Gary says. "The telegram read, 'You are a prophet.'"

Incremental, Not Monumental

These events – serving the cardinal's Mass and seeing him elected Pope – sparked in Gary a deeper fervor and devotion to the Holy Mass. Also, desire for the priesthood began to flare up in his soul. But how was he to know for sure if that was his vocation?

Father Gary, reflecting on this experience of uncertainty, recounts some insightful advice given to young people by his current bishop in the Diocese of Springfield, Massachusetts, Bishop McDonnell: "Once the bishop was giving a talk at a dinner with young people, and he said, 'For most of us – if not all of us – our call is not monumental in the sense of a dramatic call like Paul received when he got knocked off his horse, but it is more incremental. The call comes at various stages of our life, and it's those increments, those affirmations from family members, from teachers, from priests, those small acts of Providence that come at key points in life, from which we discover our call to the priesthood.'"

Sometimes when Father Gary speaks with young people, he finds that they want to hear a voice from the clouds shout,

"I want you," more or less like the Uncle Sam posters for the Army. But that's not what typically happens. He tries to tell them, "We need to be in tune with God's will through the whole host of different ways that he speaks: through other people, through religious experiences, through the small 'co-incidences' of life."

When Father Gary says this, he speaks from experience. In his own life, thoughts about the priesthood drifted in and out of his mind through the years, but he never had any huge moment where a bolt of lightning struck so that he would know definitively that God was calling him. Rather, he just had a constant desire to serve God and a conscious openness to doing whatever God asked.

In his last year of college, Gary was in a serious relationship, but he still kept wondering if God was calling him. Finally, he decided that he would never know unless he went to the seminary and spent some prolonged time in prayer. The time had come to take an active and responsible role in discerning his vocation, rather than waiting for a voice from the heavens. He remained uncertain about his vocation, but he was willing to give God the first chance. Gary made the difficult decision to break off his relationship and apply to the seminary.

From an earthly perspective, he had no assurance that he was making the right choice. Yet from the perspective of faith, he had the certitude that God, as a loving Father, would bless his courageous decision.

Here, the significance of Gary's decision should not be passed over too quickly, lest the difficulties he faced in following his vocation be smoothed over. His decision is what separates him from the "rich young man" of the Gospel and the thousand other such young men whom our Lord calls, but who turn with eyes downcast and walk away, disappointed by the difficulty his call entails. Gary cared deeply about his girlfriend, their relationship was serious, and – had he chosen otherwise – they probably would have been married. There is every reason to imagine they would have had a happy life together. Breaking up with her just on the chance that God might be calling him to something else was a very difficult decision, one of those gut-wrenching, soul-searing sorts of decisions.

This is the point – a point of great importance for any young person who is struggling to find what the Lord wants for their life: Usually God doesn't make it easy. He doesn't ask us for "make-believe" sacrifices; he asks us for real sacrifices. He doesn't make bargains, settling for us to give him 75 percent of our heart; it's all or nothing. It's demanding. It's hard. It's a vocation.

And even worse, it entails risk. That's the nature of a true call; it forces us to unclench our hands that so tightly hold onto the plans we have for our own lives. When God calls, he asks us to take a step into the unknown, to place our lives in his hands with faith, knowing it may hurt, but trusting that his will is better than our plans. God's folly is wiser than our greatest wisdom.

As Gary was in the process of carrying out his decision, the assassination attempt on John Paul II occurred. It was in May of 1981, around the time of his college graduation. For everyone at St. Mary's College, this was a horrific event. There was a psychological and emotional closeness to the Pope. He had stayed at the campus as a cardinal, and many of the priests who were professors had interacted with him. The bedroom where he stayed during his visit had a large plaque on the wall that said, "Here slept John Paul II." The big thing on campus was to swipe the "Pope's canoe" and take it out on the lake. When Mehmet Ali Agca shot the Pope in St. Peter's Square, it was a huge shock that Gary felt very personally.

But the Pope's courageous example had a deeper significance for Gary. His fortitude during the difficult recovery process and his determination to reassume his duties showed that the path God marks out for his disciples demands heroism. When Gary saw pictures of the wounded Pope, he beheld a fallen warrior, a warrior who took a bullet in the fight to spread Christ's kingdom, a warrior who would have the courage to stand again and return to the battle. In comparison, the sacrifices Gary was making in order to pursue God's will, though significant, still were small. Nearly two decades after surviving assassination, John Paul II, in his message to young people in preparation for the 16th World Youth Day, explained why sacrifice is an unavoidable part of every vocation:

Love is the condition for following [Jesus], but it is sacrifice that is the proof of that love.[29]

"If anyone wishes to come after me, let him deny himself and take up his cross daily and follow me."[30] *These words denote the radicalness of a choice that does not allow for hesitation or second thoughts. It is a demanding requirement that unsettled even the disciples and that, throughout the ages, has held back many men and women from following Christ. But it is precisely this radicalness that has also produced admirable examples of sanctity and martyrdom that strengthened and confirmed the way of the Church. Even today, these words are regarded as a stumbling block and folly.*[31] *Yet they must be faced, because the path outlined by God for his Son is the path to be undertaken by the disciple who has decided to follow Jesus. There are not two paths, but only one: the one trodden by the Master. The disciple cannot invent a different way.*

Jesus walks ahead of his followers and asks each one to do as he himself has done. He says: "I have not come to be served, but to serve; so, whoever wants to be like me must be the servant of everyone. I have come to you as one who possesses nothing; for this reason, I can ask you to leave all riches behind which prevent you from entering the kingdom of heaven. I accept denial and rejection by most of my people; therefore, I can ask you to accept denial and opposition from wherever it comes." In other words, Jesus asks that we courageously choose the same path. We have to choose it from our hearts, because external situations do not depend on us…

> *"He must deny himself." To deny oneself is to give up one's own plans that are often small and petty in order to accept God's plan. This is the path of conversion, something indispensable in a Christian life, that led St. Paul to say, "It is no longer I who live, but Christ who lives in me."*[32, 33]

Strengthened in his resolve by the Holy Father's example of love proven through sacrifice, Gary followed through with his resolution and entered the seminary in the fall of 1981.

As his years in the seminary progressed, his struggles did not cease, but gradually Gary's vocation to the priesthood did come more clearly into focus. In retrospect, he has no doubt whatsoever that this is the path the Lord wanted, and now after many wonderful years as a priest, he continues constantly to thank God for granting him the grace and strength to say "Yes."

Heroes

For Father Gary, John Paul II seemed more than real; he was bigger than life. His holiness and the way he spoke the truth was something that Father Gary wanted to model in his own life. "How amazing it is that the leader of our church could walk into countries with dictators and look them in the face and tell them to stop oppressing their people," he says, "or that he could come to the United States and challenge a president about the dignity of life. Who else in the world, either as a head of state or as a moral leader could say what he said? Some kids idolize an athlete or a rock star, but for me, the Pope was my hero. Meeting him meant a whole lot to me."

As a newly ordained priest, Father Gary had the chance to concelebrate Mass with the Pope at Castel Gandolfo on the feast of St. Maximilian Kolbe, August 16, 1987. The experience was unbelievable. Father Gary had changed profoundly since he served as acolyte for Cardinal Wojtyla at St. Peter's tomb nearly a decade earlier. Now, at the inmost heart of his being, Father Gary shared a permanent bond with the Pope. Now he shared in Christ's priesthood; now he too was a custodian of the Church's sacred mysteries, charged to stand as "another Christ," and endowed with the power to transform bread and wine into Christ's body and blood.

Awareness of that reality's magnitude was overwhelming. "I was standing there, extending my hand, concelebrating Mass with the Pope, and just trembling," recalls Father Gary. "When I approached the altar and took the cup of precious blood in my quivering hands, the Holy Father was right beside me."

After Mass, Father Gary knelt before the Pope and presented him with a picture drawn by the children at Sacred Heart School where he was the associate pastor. He had told the children that he was going to Rome and would be meeting the Pope. They made a drawing depicting John Paul II and an image of the Sacred Heart of Jesus, and underneath they wrote, "Pope John Paul II, we love you – the children of

Sacred Heart School." Father Gary handed the picture to the Pontiff and conversed briefly in Polish. The Pope asked what the children had written, and Father Gary read the message aloud. The Pope replied, "And you tell the children that the Pope loves them, too." The Pope passed the picture to Msgr. Dziwisz, and turned to walk away. After taking a few steps, he stopped in his tracks, turned back around to face Father Gary, and held up his finger, saying, "God bless America." Then he walked away.

"It was awesome, just awesome," says Father Gary. "When I was in his presence, I had the exact feeling that people in Palestine must have felt when Jesus was walking in their midst. There couldn't have been any difference when John Paul II walked near me. You just wanted to touch him because you knew you were touching holiness. I was convinced back in 1987 when I met him that this man was going to be a saint; I knew I had just touched a saint."

"If you have a hero, for example if you admire a sports star, you want an autographed bat, or a football, or a jersey. That's how I felt with John Paul II. Everyone laughs at me because I have John Paul II memorabilia all over the rectory, like a museum: statues, figurines, pictures, clocks, medals, books. I could open my own JP II museum. The housekeeper at my previous rectory used to ask jokingly, 'What will you find next?' I have encased in my office one of the Holy Father's zucchettos; and together with my chalice, it is my prized possession. Msgr. Dziwisz sent it, and on the back is inscribed 'JP II, 10-10-2003,' the date of the 25th anniversary of his election."

Beyond Good-Bye

The final time Father Gary saw John Paul II was in August of 2004, less than a year before his death. A picture of that occasion hangs above his desk, and whenever he looks at it, it gives him strength and encouragement.

Father Gary, now serving as the vocation director for the Diocese of Springfield, Massachusetts, was in Rome with his friend and predecessor, Father Christopher Malatesta, the former vocation director. They had rented a small car and decided to drive to the village of Castel Gandolfo, where the Pope spends part of his summer in escape from the city's heat. Father Gary knew the general direction but wasn't exactly sure how to get there. However, outside Rome he spotted a car full of nuns and decided to follow them, correctly guessing that they were headed to the Pope's Wednesday audience.

By the time they arrived in Castel Gandolfo, parked the car, and went to the plaza in front of the Pope's residence, the Swiss Guards had already closed the gates because the crowd was at capacity. But, after a few minutes, they let an additional dozen people squeeze in, and Father Gary was among them.

Remarkably, from a distance Father Gary recognized a Polish Dominican, the same priest who had arranged for him to celebrate Mass with the Pope in 1987. So he waded through the crowd to reach him. That priest told Father Gary that he could greet the Pope if he wanted, gave him a sticky note with a Vatican stamp on it, and told him to stand with a group of pilgrims from Krakow. "So the audience continued," remembers Father Gary, "and of course the Pope was suffering badly at the time. He spoke with difficulty, and it was hard to understand him. You just felt awful to see him suffering."

Yet everyone knew that the way the Pope bore his suffering was a revelation of his deep union with Christ's redeeming cross. He was participating mysteriously in Christ's redemptive work by suffering together with Christ, a topic he had meditated upon in his 1984 Apostolic Letter on the meaning of Christian suffering:

> *While the first great chapter of the Gospel of suffering is written down, as the generations pass, by those who suffer persecutions for Christ's sake, simultaneously another great chapter of this Gospel unfolds through the course of history. This chapter is written by all those who suffer together with Christ, uniting their human sufferings to his salvific suffering...*
>
> *Down through the centuries and generations it has been seen that in suffering there is concealed a particular power that draws a person interiorly close to Christ, a special grace... When this body is gravely ill, totally incapacitated, and the person is almost incapable of living and acting, all the more do interior maturity and spiritual greatness become evident, constituting a touching lesson to those who are healthy and normal.*

This interior maturity and spiritual greatness in suffering are certainly the result of a particular conversion and cooperation with the grace of the crucified Redeemer. It is he himself who acts at the heart of human sufferings through his Spirit of truth, through the consoling Spirit. It is he who transforms, in a certain sense, the very substance of the spiritual life, indicating for the person who suffers a place close to himself. It is he – as the interior Master and Guide – who reveals to the suffering brother and sister this wonderful interchange, situated at the very heart of the mystery of the redemption. Suffering is, in itself, an experience of evil. But Christ has made suffering the firmest basis of the definitive good, namely the good of eternal salvation. By his suffering on the cross, Christ reached the very roots of evil, of sin, and of death. He conquered the author of evil, Satan, and his permanent rebellion against the Creator. To the suffering brother or sister Christ discloses and gradually reveals the horizons of the Kingdom of God: the horizons of a world converted to the Creator, of a world free from sin, a world being built on the saving power of love. And slowly but effectively, Christ leads into this world, into this kingdom of the Father, suffering man, in a certain sense through the very heart of his suffering. For suffering cannot be transformed and changed by a grace from outside, but from within…

… For it is above all a call. It is a vocation. Christ does not explain in the abstract the reasons for suffering, but before all else he says: "Follow me!" Come! Take part through your suffering in this work of saving the world, a salvation achieved

> *through my suffering, through my cross! Gradually, as the individual takes up his cross, spiritually uniting himself to the cross of Christ, the salvific meaning of suffering is revealed before him. He does not discover this meaning at his own human level, but at the level of the suffering of Christ. At the same time, however, from this level of Christ the salvific meaning of suffering descends to man's level and becomes, in a sense, the individual's personal response. It is then that man finds in his suffering interior peace and even spiritual joy.*[34]

As the Holy Father's audience ended, the group of pilgrims from Krakow marched onto the platform to greet the Pope, and Father Gary and his traveling companion were among them. He remembers, "When I went to the platform where the Holy Father was, I asked Bishop Stanislaw Dziwisz, in Polish, if we could kneel in front of the Holy Father for his blessing, and he waved his hand to indicate for us to go in front of the Pope's chair."

Kneeling before the Pope, they waited as the Holy Father raised his arm with effort and gave his blessing. That picture hangs in Father Gary's office. As it was taken, he knew he would never see the Holy Father again in this life, and indeed, before summer's return, John Paul II closed his eyes in final rest.

But in a way that is just the beginning of the story.

"We are beginning to see after his death that he is even more powerful now that he is in heaven," Father Gary says.

"In my mind, there is no doubt that John Paul the Great will do even more after his death than he did in life."

From his standpoint as vocation director, Father Gary is beginning to see tremendous fruit; he sees young men and young women responding to God's call unlike before. He says that part of that is because people are reading anew John Paul's works—his teachings, his encyclicals, his letters. "Everyone wants to grab a hold of his writings," he says. "While John Paul was alive, it was one thing, but now, after his death his works are in a way even more valuable."

Yet, beyond the lasting effects of his written works, Father Gary believes that the Pope's intercession from heaven is phenomenal. He believes that he has experienced this firsthand. Privately, he often entrusts his vocation work and particular individuals to John Paul's care. In the fall of 2006, his diocese had a total of thirteen seminarians in all years of study combined. The next year, that number nearly doubled. When I last spoke to him in spring of 2008, he already had twelve new applications for the fall. It is a promising increase for a diocese with only 250,000 Catholics.

During the years after John Paul's death, Father Gary has witnessed the number of seminarians go from seven, to thirteen, to twenty-two, and next fall there will likely be around thirty. The diocese has not had that number in many, many years. "Part of that is due to the intercession of John Paul the Great, there is no question in my mind," he says. "I also credit the fact that when I began my work as vocation director we opened up an Adoration for Vocations chapel in Ludlow, Massachussets, with the approval and blessing of Bishop McDonnell. When we opened that chapel we had seven seminarians, and now we could have thirty by the fall of 2008. We had four young women enter into religious life. The monstrance in the chapel was brought to Rome… and on the feast of St. Andrew in 2004, November 30th, the monstrance was blessed by Pope John Paul II with the intention of [being used for] prayer for vocations. That monstrance and the presence of our Eucharistic Lord, along with the intercession of Pope John Paul II, has been the instrumental reason for our increase in vocations."

In a sense, John Paul could be said to have a special stake in these young vocations. "These young people coming forward in their late teens and early twenties have been influenced by him," Father Gary reflects. "They have been present at World Youth Days; they have been exposed to his teachings for all their life, and that has made a tremendous difference – they are truly the JPII generation. Now, John Paul the Great is looking after all these young people from heaven."

FATHER GARY DAILEY *is director of vocations for the Diocese of Springfield, Massachusetts.*

Chapter 6
UPON THIS ROCK

A Prayer in Stone

Centuries of pilgrim footsteps have pressed and polished the intricate marble floor of St. Peter's Basilica, etching in stone a memory of their devout passage. If one glances about the basilica's interior, the sight is nearly too much to take in, nearly dizzying. Every nook and cranny is filled with statuary and sculpture, art and artwork, paintings and mosaics, bronze and gold and silver. Even the floor itself is a work of art, a symphony of stone, a visual concert. Slabs of mottled rose and marmoreal grey blend in lithic harmony with teal and white and pearl. The floor is solid; it is unyielding. It grounds the whole panorama and supports the spectacle towering above and around. It is the expansive foundation of a prayer wrought in stone.

Bishop Peter Jugis lay face down on that ancient floor on June 12th, 1983, breathing in the dusty aroma of a red woven rug which separated his nose from the cool stones below. As he lay there, filled with emotion, the choir echoed a long litany of saints, imploring intercession from the great Christians of old. *Sancta Maria Mater Dei, ora pro nobis. Sancte Ioseph, ora pro nobis. Sancti Petre et Paule, orate pro nobis.* Holy Mary, Mother of God, pray for us. St. Joseph, pray for us. Sts. Peter and Paul, pray for us.

In that liturgy, the gathered assembly of families, friends, and faithful begged all the angels and saints of heaven to join in praying for the young men lying face down on the carpet. They prayed that those men would be loyal, that they would be holy, that they would be priests after Christ's own heart, that they would be pillars rooted firm upon a foundation of rock. John Paul II commented on the significance of that moment for a priest:

> *As we ponder the birth of our priesthood…each of us recalls that most evocative moment when, on the day of our priestly ordination, we prostrated ourselves on the sanctuary floor. This gesture of deep humility and obedient openness was splendidly designed to ready our soul for the sacramental imposition of hands, through which the Holy Spirit entered us to accomplish his work. Once we had risen from the floor, we knelt before the*

bishop to be ordained priests, and our hands were anointed by him for the celebration of the Holy Sacrifice…[35]

As his own ordination ceremony continued, Bishop Jugis tried to ingrain deep in his memory the precise place where he became a priest, the place where he knelt as John Paul II pressed his hands upon his head and called down the Holy Spirit, the place where his soul was changed for all eternity. "When I make return visits to Rome I always make it a point to go back to St. Peter's just to stand on that spot and remember that it was here that my priesthood began," Bishop Jugis says. "I felt very blessed to have that opportunity to be ordained by the Holy Father. It was during the Holy Year of Redemption and I will always remember what he said to us in his homily."

Beloved brothers, during the years of my service as a bishop, one of the moments of most intense joy, and no less of trepidation, was that in which, by means of the imposition of my hands, I ordained new priests for the church community. I experience equal joy and trepidation today, in this solemn ordination, which reaches completion at the tomb of Peter during the Jubilee of the Redemption. You will be priests of the 1950th anniversary of the Redemption. If such an event signifies for all believers an urgent invitation to meditate on their own life and on their own Christian vocation in light of the mystery of redemption, such an invitation is addressed in a special way

> *to all those who are and who will be – as you will be in a few moments – "ministers of Christ and administrators of the mysteries of God."*[36, 37]

"In a way, that theme marks my priesthood as one of ministry of Christ's redemptive mercy, love, and compassion," says Bishop Jugis.

Foundation of a Vocation

As Bishop Jugis recounts the story, the origin of his vocation was very simple. There was no voice from heaven, no fanfare or dramatic episode. Rather, he traces the beginning of his vocation to two factors: an interior discontentment with humdrum life and a chance encounter with a parish priest. "I was a college student at the University of North Carolina at Charlotte," he explains. "I was studying accounting, and doing very well, making good grades. But at about twenty years of age, I found out that this work really was not fulfilling. I sat myself down and said, 'Well, I'm smart enough to make good grades and to succeed intellectually, but this cannot be my life's work. I can't do this!' So I started looking for something that would nourish me interiorly, something I could put myself into completely.

"Around that time, I was playing the organ for a wedding Mass at one of the neighboring parishes, and after the Mass the priest came up to me. He just asked me if I had ever thought about being a priest. I told him, 'No, I hadn't.' And his next line was, 'Well, think about it, will you?' and then he turned and walked back to the sacristy. That was what planted the seed and got me started thinking seriously about the priesthood. I consider it a real blessing."

After letting the idea stew in the back of his mind for a whole year, Bishop Jugis decided to tell his parents that he thought God wanted him to be a priest. To his surprise, they said they had suspected he was gravitating in that direction, but they didn't want to interfere. They wanted him to arrive at a conclusion on his own.

"That was a tremendous confirmation of what I had been trying to discern interiorly for many months," Bishop Jugis says. "I began taking some philosophy courses at the university in order to get the prerequisites to begin theology. Then I approached the vocation director and asked how to become a seminarian in the diocese. To my surprise, the vocation director said that the bishop would seriously consider sending me to Rome to study at the North American College. I had no dream or expectation of that happening, but in August of 1979 I began studying theology as a twenty-two-year-old, right out of college."

Peter's Successor

When Bishop Jugis arrived in Rome, John Paul II had been Pope for less than a year. "I thought that the Holy Spirit was sending some special message to the church," he says, "and I found it very interesting, very novel, and it was worth paying attention to see what this was all about... By then, I knew that I wanted to be a priest, and what this new, young Pope was saying with so much vitality and energy caused me to be more excited and interested at the prospect of holy orders."

Soon thereafter, in February of 1980, John Paul came to visit the seminarians at the North American College as part of his effort to visit all the national seminary colleges. "I still remember that first time when I met the Pope," remarks Bishop Jugis. "All the seminarians were lined up along the wall, and he was coming down and greeting everyone. As he came to me, I said, 'Your Holiness, I pray for you every day.' Apparently he didn't hear or understand me at first, so he looked at me with a puzzled expression and asked, 'What?' I repeated again, 'Your Holiness, I pray for you every day,' and that is when he placed his hand on my shoulder and kind of shook me and said, 'God bless you!'"

For Bishop Jugis, the time he spent in Rome was a special opportunity to be close to the Vicar of Christ. He never let an opportunity to encounter the Pope slip by. "Whenever the Vatican office in charge of papal ceremonies would send notification to our college requesting seminarians to serve the Pope's Mass, I volunteered every single time," says Bishop Jugis, "I wasn't chosen every time, but in several instances I was. Once I was the acolyte who held his miter. I also remember the Corpus Christi procession in 1982. I was one of the deacons chosen to help hold the baldacchino over the Holy

Father as he carried the monstrance from St. John Lateran to St. Mary Major. I was just amazed at the blessings I received from God, being right next to the Holy Father, an arm's length away for the whole length of the procession down the road between the two basilicas. What a blessing that was to be so close to him and to be so close to the Blessed Sacrament."

A Young Shepherd

In 2004, Bishop Jugis joyfully remembered the experiences he had in Rome as a seminarian, culminating in his priestly ordination. He again stood in St. Peter's Basilica and walked across the floor until he reached the place where his priesthood began, at the Pope's hands, more than twenty years prior. But on this occasion, he came to Rome under very different circumstances. He had been summoned for his first official *ad limina* visit, the pilgrimage bishops are required to make every five years to give the Holy Father an official account of their diocese.

Only a few months had passed since he was appointed bishop of his native Diocese of Charlotte, North Carolina. "It was a special blessing to be chosen to be a bishop by the same Pope that ordained me a priest. The Pope does have personal input in the choosing of the bishops; he gets to make the final decision. I was quite moved that he chose me. He probably didn't recognize my name, but when he saw that I had been ordained by him, I hope he felt proud – glad to see that I had turned out well."

Bishop Jugis had a few minutes alone with the Holy Father there in his study to make his *ad limina* report.

At one moment while they were alone, the Pope looked at him and said, "You are very young."

Bishop Jugis replied, "Yes, your Holiness, I am." Bishop Jugis was forty-six when he was named, one of the youngest bishops at that time.

Then the Pope started reminiscing, "You know, when I was named bishop, I was thirty-eight. I was much younger!"

Bishop Jugis says, "I realized later, when I read *[Rise, Let Us Be on Our Way]*, the autobiographical book that the Pope had been dictating the summer before, that his early years as a bishop in Poland were uppermost on his mind. He probably made the connection to me, and related my youthful appearance – although I was not thirty-eight – to his first years as a bishop starting out in Poland."

In that memoir, John Paul II recounts the conversation he had with the primate of Poland, Cardinal Sefan Wyszynski, when the cardinal informed him of the Holy See's decision.

The youthful bishop-to-be said, "Your Eminence, I am too young; I'm only thirty-eight."

But the primate wisely replied, "That is a weakness which can soon be remedied."[38]

At first, Bishop Karol Wojtyla was embarrassed by his youthfulness compared to the older bishops whom he revered.[39] But he quickly passed beyond that initial embarrassment and distinguished himself as an outstanding and fearless shepherd amid the difficulties posed by Communism in Poland during those years.

Bishop Jugis has taken to heart several elements of the Holy Father's pastoral approach. In the first respect, he has embraced the Holy Father's example of availability. "The Pope was extremely available, showing his love for people by sharing his time with them," says Bishop Jugis. "I try to emulate that in my own pastoral work. As a parish priest I did, and also as a bishop now. I know what it meant to me, as a mere seminarian, to come into personal contact with the Pope. I found that incredible. It made an impression and motivated me to do likewise, to make myself available to the people of my parish and later to the people of my diocese."

"The Pope gave you a lot of time. He never gave the impression that he was rushed or wanted to be done with you quickly, though he certainly had a lot to do. But even at my ordination, I have pictures of him with my own bishop, Bishop Begley. The Pope took the time before the Mass began to visit with all the different people who were part of that ceremony. These, and many other small things the Holy Father did, combined to create a spirit of accessibility and availability which has influenced my own pastoral approach."

A second direct influence of John Paul II arose from his proclamation of the Year of the Eucharist, starting in 2004. "I felt that as a personal mandate from the Pope," Bishop Jugis recalls.

The Holy Father had written to bishops about his hopes for the Year of the Eucharist:

> *My brother bishops will certainly understand that this initiative…is meant to take place on a deeply spiritual level… The Year of the Eucharist has its source in the amazement with which the church contemplates this great mystery. It is an amazement which I myself constantly experience…As I look forward to the twenty-seventh year of my Petrine ministry, I consider it a great grace to be able to call the whole church to contemplate, praise, and adore in a special way this ineffable sacrament. May the Year of the Eucharist be for everyone a precious opportunity to grow in awareness of the incomparable treasure which Christ has entrusted to his church.*[40]

John Paul II never reached his twenty-seventh year of ministry; he was destined to leave this world on April 2, 2005, and a new pontiff would preside over the closing of the Year of the Eucharist. Nonetheless, Bishop Jugis enthusiastically took the Pope's message to heart. "In honor of the Holy Father," he says, "and in honor of the year of the Eucharist which he had given as a gift to the church, I wanted to do something special in our diocese. We came up with the idea of sponsoring, promoting, and putting on a Eucharistic Congress. The Congress was held around the end of the Year of the Eucharist, in October of 2005. It was so successful – it was the first time that anything like that had been done in the

Charlotte Diocese – that we decided to continue the tradition, and it is a lasting legacy of the Pope's influence on me and of his love for the Eucharist. This fall, in 2009, we are going to have our fifth annual Eucharistic Congress. The people have received it so well, and the numbers attending increase every year."

Stories of such success are heartening to hear. The Church is alive in Charlotte! No doubt, the love of Christ impels this energetic bishop and his flourishing diocese. From heaven, John Paul II must smile to see that he chose a good shepherd.

A Brick between the Eyes

Except for the black suit and collar, Father David Toups looks like he ought to have a surfboard in hand, basking in the sun, instead of standing in front of a theology class at St. Vincent de Paul Regional Seminary in Boynton Beach, Florida (where he taught for three years before being whisked off to Washington, D.C., to serve as associate director for the United States Conference of Catholic Bishops Secretariat of Clergy, Consecrated Life, and Vocations). Yet behind his smiling face, sandy hair, and misty-grey eyes, lies an extraordinary story.

As a little boy, back when he was just David, he told his mother, "I either want to be a priest or a lawyer." Of course, she was probably thinking, "Oh boy, a priest or a lawyer, kind of opposite ends of the spectrum." But she never pressured him or tried to turn him one way or the other.

Theirs was what you could call a traditional Catholic family, even though nowadays such families are all too often not the tradition. David was the youngest of three children, and for them the faith was a normal part of life. They went to Mass as a family every Sunday, David was an altar server, and he grew to admire the priests at the parish.

But as the years progressed and David got older, thoughts of becoming a priest dwindled (as so often is the case), and thoughts of being an attorney increased – no doubt accompanied by thoughts of red sports cars, beach houses, bodacious babes, killer parties, fame, fortune – a teenage boy's typical daydreams. So after high school, David decided to enroll at Florida Southern College, just east of Tampa, and soon was in the thick of campus life, caught up in all the attractions the world has to offer.

What more could David want? He was pre-law, making good grades, having a blast on the weekends, popular at his fraternity, and even got elected president of his class. College life had filled his cup with sweet wine; why not drain it to the dregs and go back for more? Still, throughout this period, if anyone had asked the question, he would have affirmed without hesitation that his Catholic faith was important. But from the outside, the truth of that affirmation was difficult to perceive.

Then, like a ton of bricks, came a wake-up call.

During the summer between sophomore and junior year of college, David got into a serious conversation about religion with a girl who was one of his dear friends. Eventually, the talk got a bit heated, and she retorted, "You know, you call yourself a Catholic and a Christian, but you are really not living the faith...so you're actually some kind of a hypocrite, huh?"

That accusation was like getting smashed with a brick between the eyeballs. But what could David say? She was right.

If he believed all the things that he claimed to believe, if he thought the faith was true – and he did – then why wasn't he embracing it fully? His friend had thrown down the gauntlet; it was time to stand up like a real man and take ownership of his Catholic faith. But that meant facing its challenges without squirming or wimping out, and that was going to be hard.

Francis Did It; I Can Too

During that same summer, David was working as an intern for the public defender's office. Each morning he would drive over to the county prison to speak with the inmates who faced court charges. The irony was that now he felt like the one who had been caught. He had been playing a con game for too long; others could be fooled, but his own conscience knew the fraud. The time had come for change.

So, before going to the jail for work, David started attending daily Mass. He started praying the Rosary, studying the Bible, and reading about the saints. Also, quite importantly, he returned to the sacrament of reconciliation, and for the first time as an adult man experienced the freedom and joy which that sacrament brings, when God's awesome power obliterates our darkest sins. But hand-in-hand with this experience of conversion, David was also experiencing in an increasingly perceptible way, a call to more complete commitment. The Lord was at work in his soul, beckoning for an answer.

One day David picked up a book on the life of St. Francis, and he could not help seeing a parallel to his own life. Here was a frivolous young man, basically an upper-middle-class partier like himself, who managed to turn his life around dramatically. Moreover, St. Francis' experience of conversion drove him to share that experience of Christ's love and peace with everyone he encountered. Eventually, St. Francis laid the foundation for the Church's largest religious order, inspiring droves of Franciscans through the centuries to cast aside earthly riches for the sake of eternal treasure. The example St. Francis gave by living a life wholly consecrated to God was countercultural in 11th century, and it remains countercultural today. John Paul II remarked of the saint:

> *By his life Francis proclaimed and continues to proclaim today the saving word of the Gospel. It is difficult to find a saint whose message could withstand so deeply "the test of time." Francis is the saint who is, in a certain sense, universal; through him Christ wanted to proclaim the Gospel not only to his era*

> *but to others as well, to our own age, to cultures and civilizations very different from one another.*[41]

The enduring power of St. Francis example stems from the way he lived out a life consecrated to God by the vows of poverty, chastity, and obedience. In our own time, consecrated men and women continue to challenge all Christians to strive for greater holiness by making Christ visible in a unique way. John Paul II explained:

> *By the profession of the evangelical counsels the characteristic features of Jesus – the chaste, poor and obedient one – are made constantly "visible" in the midst of the world and the eyes of the faithful are directed towards the mystery of the kingdom of God already at work in history, even as it awaits its full realization in heaven.*
>
> *In every age there have been men and women who, obedient to the Father's call and to the prompting of the Spirit, have chosen this special way of following Christ, in order to devote themselves to him with an "undivided" heart.*[42] *Like the Apostles, they too have left everything behind in order to be with Christ and to put themselves, as he did, at the service of God and their brothers and sisters.*[43]

The Pope himself, as a young man, was deeply attracted by the consecrated life, especially through the writings of St. John of the Cross, the great Carmelite reformer and mystic.

Still, young Karol Wojtyla eventually saw, with the guidance of Cardinal Stefan Sapieha who was directing Krakow's clandestine seminary during the dangerous years of Poland's Nazi occupation, that the Lord was calling him to strive for holiness by following another path – the vocation to diocesan priesthood.

In like manner, St. Francis' example of wholehearted devotion to Christ made its impression on David. He started thinking to himself, "If Francis could have the grace of God to leave everything behind, then perhaps I could do the same. If God gave St. Francis the strength to do it, then he'll give me the strength, too."

However, David had no illusions about becoming another St. Francis; he could tell that God was not calling him to the consecrated life. Yet, reading the saint's story was an important part of his journey toward the priesthood. It challenged him to give his life more generously to the Lord, to respond to the unique vocation God had crafted for him from all eternity. "Deep in my heart," he says, "I kept hearing that call of the apostles, leave everything behind, drop your nets and follow me. So that summer I broke up with my girlfriend, resigned from my offices at the fraternity and the university, and applied to the college seminary." In the fall of 1991, he was accepted as a seminarian for the Diocese of St. Petersburg, and began studying philosophy at St. John Vianney College Seminary in Miami.

As the years progressed, David came to see John Paul II as the ideal model of a diocesan priest, a role model whom he strove to emulate. Still, like the Holy Father himself, David continued to be enriched, encouraged, and challenged by the example of men and women who had given their hearts to Christ in the consecrated life. Among them, Mother Teresa and her Missionaries of Charity are salient examples, but more on that in a moment.

A Model to Follow

Just after completing his second year of philosophy, David encountered John Paul II in person for the first time. He was preparing to go to Rome to start studying theology, but, prior to departing, he attended World Youth Day in Denver as a youth group chaperone. There he heard the Pope speak, and in the distance about twenty-five football fields away, scarcely visible, he beheld a millimeter tall white speck – John Paul II.

Despite the distance, the experience was intense – being there with nearly a million other young people, praying with them and chanting with them, "JAY-PEA-TWO, we-love-you." The Pope was electric, interacting with the crowd and echoing back, "JAY-PEA-TWO loves you, too!"

The whole event was brimming with energy and vitality; after all, the theme was taken from John 10:10: "I came so that they might have life, and have it more abundantly." John Paul was a convincing messenger who kept communicating this message to young people throughout his entire pontificate, a message of Jesus Christ, a message of liberation, hope, joy, and light. United to Christ, we have life in abundance.

But little did David know he would soon encounter the Pope again at a much closer distance. About a month after arriving in Rome, his class of seminarians residing at the North American College was invited to pray the Rosary with the Holy Father. Now, rather than seeing the Pope from afar, lost in a sea of thousands, David was able to pray with the Pope in an intimate setting, glimpsing the interior life of this spiritual giant up close.

Upon This Rock

With a candle in hand, on June 29, 1994, David stood flanking the ambo in St. Peter's basilica, where the book of the Gospel lay open to Matthew 16. A deacon, vested in the blood-scarlet of martyrs, incensed the Gospel, sending puffs of white smoke drifting gently into the expanse of the basilica's vast dome. Then the deacon began to read, chanting the Gospel in melodious Latin, mingling his song sweetly with the lingering incense: *"Tu es Petrus et super hanc petram aedificabo ecclesiam meam et portae inferi non praevalebunt adversum eam."*

David, standing beside the deacon, and only a few feet from the Pope, could read that same inscription, written in letters circling inside the basilica's dome. That verse, Matthew 16:18, reports Christ's words as he placed upon Peter's shoulders the colossal responsibility of being the first Pope, "And so I say to you, you are Peter, and upon this rock I will build my Church, and the gates of the netherworld shall not prevail against it."

Father David retains vivid memories of that scene, on the Feast of Sts. Peter and Paul, standing in that sacred basilica built above the very bones of St. Peter himself, standing in the presence of Peter's successor, John Paul II, and hearing the words of that Gospel. The awesome magnitude of the office of Peter, and the ponderous weight of the Church's 2000 years seemed condensed into a single moment.

"After that, one cannot be the same," Father David says, "One cannot look at the Holy Father in the same way, knowing the gravity of his office and the grace of God that accompanies him." The office of Peter is the office of a good shepherd, and a good shepherd must lay down his life for his sheep. John Paul II prayed often that young people would share in bearing the burden of that mission:

> *Good Shepherd…teach the young people of the world, the meaning of "laying down" their lives through vocation and mission. Just as you sent the Apostles to preach the Gospel to the ends of the earth, so now challenge the youth of the Church to carry on the vast mission of making you known to all those who have not yet heard of you! Give these young people the courage and generosity of the great missionaries of the past so that, through the witness of their faith and their solidarity with every brother and sister in need, the world may*

discover the Truth, the Goodness, and the Beauty of the Life you alone can give.[44]

St. Peter, as the first Pope, surrendered his life, crucified upon a cross. But, considering himself unworthy to die in the same manner as Our Lord, he begged the executioners to fasten him to the cross upside down. Now his nail-pierced bones rest beneath the basilica's central altar, canopied by the massive bronze baldacchino Bernini wrought. John Paul II likewise suffered for his flock in a manner different than our Lord, first surviving assassination, and later accepting crucifixion upon the slow cross of illness. Now his final resting place is also in the crypt of that ancient basilica, where thousands of pilgrims come in seemingly endless procession to pray at his tomb.

Beauty of Simplicity

At the time of John Paul II's death, many people were surprised to learn about the great simplicity and frugality with which he had lived. Through all the years, he remained at heart a simple Polish priest. He was a man with a deeply mystical interior life, burdened with the weight and worries of the office of Peter, yet he found great joy in the simple things: the smile of a child, a lighthearted moment with old friends, the smell of roasted Polish sausages doused in liquor and served flaming.

A priest who once dined with the Holy Father at a public banquet told me this anecdote. At the end of the meal, a specially prepared cake was served, a traditional Polish recipe that was the Holy Father's favorite. At this time, the Holy Father already had to watch his health, and one of the nuns who took care of the papal household was present to keep an eye on the Pope's diet. When the cake was offered, she made eye contact with the person serving the cake, and held her fingers slightly apart to indicate the proper sized sliver to serve the Pope. But when the Pope saw out of the corner of his eye that "Sister dietician" had turned away, he motioned to the waiter, placed his hand on the waiter's hand, and with an impish grin positioned the knife to cut a much more ample slice.

John Paul II was a man surrounded by the splendor of palaces and grand basilicas, but he never grew attached to those things. He had little to call his own. Many commentators were struck by a line in the Holy Father's last will and testament: "I leave no possessions of which it will be necessary to dispose. As for the things I use every day, I ask that they be distributed as seems appropriate."[45]

Unsurprisingly, the Holy Father felt a special relationship with those other simple souls, who lived with their hearts wholly given to Christ. Mother Teresa was the most outstanding of those kindred spirits. She was someone with whom John Paul could relate at the deepest level. After returning from a ten-day pilgrimage to India in February of 1986, during which he saw Mother Teresa's work in Calcutta, he resolved to establish a hospice run by her Missionaries of Charity *inside the Vatican,* quite a resolution given the Vatican's small acreage. When the hospice was opened two years later in a renovated building on the edge of the tiny Vatican City State, it was dubbed "Dono di Maria" (the "Gift of Mary") House. This extraordinary gesture revealed the extent of the Holy Father's admiration for the "saint of Calcutta." In his eyes, she was an outstanding example of a consecrated life lived to the full, a beacon of light shining amid the world's gloom.[46]

At Mother Teresa's beatification in 2003, he acknowledged to a crowd of pilgrims gathered for the occasion, "I was bound to her by deep esteem and sincere affection… there is no doubt that the new Blessed was one of the greatest missionaries of the twentieth century."[47] As he continued, he described the aspects of the holy woman's example that affected him the most, posing the question:

> *Where did Mother Teresa find the strength to place herself completely at the service of others? She found it in prayer and in the silent contemplation of Jesus Christ, his Holy Face, his Sacred Heart. She herself said as much: "The fruit of silence is prayer; the fruit of prayer is faith; the fruit of faith is love; the fruit of love is service; the fruit of service is peace." Peace, even at the side of the dying, even in nations at war, even in the face of attacks and hostile criticism. It was prayer that filled her heart with Christ's own peace and enabled her to radiate that peace to others.*

> *. . . Her very smile was a "yes" to life, a joyful "yes," born of profound faith and love, a "yes" purified in the crucible of suffering. She renewed that "yes" each morning, in union with Mary, at the foot of Christ's cross. The "thirst" of the crucified Jesus became Mother Teresa's own thirst and the inspiration of her path of holiness.*
>
> *. . . However, today more than ever, Mother Teresa's message is an invitation addressed to us all. Her entire existence reminds us that* being Christian means being witnesses of charity. *This is what the new Blessed entrusts to us. Echoing her words, I urge each one to follow generously and courageously in the footsteps of this authentic disciple of Christ. On the path of charity, Mother Teresa walks at your side.*[48]

Her testimony was made even more remarkable by the long period of spiritual darkness she experienced, a suffering which only came to public knowledge after her death:

> *Her greatness lies in her ability to give without counting the cost, to give "until it hurts." Her life was a radical living and a bold proclamation of the Gospel.*
>
> *. . .Mother Teresa shared in the passion of the crucified Christ in a special way during long years of "inner darkness." For her, that was a test, at times an agonizing one, which she accepted as a rare "gift and privilege."*
>
> *In the darkest hours she clung even more tenaciously to prayer before the Blessed Sacrament. This harsh spiritual trial led her to*

identify herself more and more closely with those whom she served each day, feeling their pain and, at times, even their rejection.[49]

Like John Paul II, Father David was touched by his encounters with Mother Teresa. By living her consecrated life to the point of heroism, she challenged everyone who crossed her path to strive for a more perfect love of Christ. "When a person meets someone like that, his life is changed," says Father David. "You can't help but strive for greater holiness in your own life."

While still a seminarian, Father David had worked with Mother Teresa's Missionaries of Charity, helping out at their shelters in Rome. Later on, as a priest, he would lead her sisters in prayer, Mass, and holy hours. So he knew the Missionaries of Charity well.

His most memorable meeting with Mother Teresa was on the Feast of the Immaculate Conception, December 8, 1993. Mother Teresa had come to the Missionaries of Charity house in Rome to receive the final vows of the sisters who were making their perpetual profession. David happened to be accompanied by another seminarian, now Father Ken Malley, and they had no idea that she was going to be there. At first, they walked right through the entrance of the convent, and scarcely noticed a tiny little sister in a blue and white sari, with a dark blue sweater, standing at the front gate. But a moment later, Ken took a second look, and gasped, "That's Mother Teresa!"

So both of them went scrambling back and knelt down to greet her – anyone who has seen her knows she was tiny, hardly over four feet tall. Mother Teresa took out two miraculous medals – these are medals impressed on one side with an image of the Blessed Virgin Mary surrounded by stars. She kissed the medals, and handed one to each of them. Then she turned and went inside.

Mother Knows Best

After the sisters' profession ceremony, all the guests and families who had come were leaving, so that the sisters could have some time alone with Mother Teresa. But David and Ken still needed to pray their holy hour that day, so they asked one of the sisters if it was all right to stay a while longer in the chapel. She said, "Oh sure, stay as long as you want," and they went into the chapel to pray.

In the Missionary of Charity chapels, you always take your shoes off in the presence of the Blessed Sacrament, in the presence of the Lord. The practice originated in India, where Mother Teresa founded the Missionaries, but it coincides wonderfully with scriptural images. You can imagine Moses, approaching the burning bush, being commanded to remove his sandals in the Lord's presence, for he trod upon sacred ground.

Anyway, there David and Ken were, shoes off, in stocking feet, praying in the chapel, when suddenly a sister came in and tapped them on the shoulder and said, "Hello brothers, Mother is right outside if you would like to speak with her."

They looked at each other, thinking, "If *we* would like to speak with her? Absolutely! Yes!" They went running out into the cold December air, standing on the cobblestones in their socks, waiting to see Mother Teresa.

Mother Teresa never minced any words, and at times her courageous candor sparked controversy (for example, her famous comments at the United Nations in defense of the unborn). On this occasion, she had one message in mind as she lifted her little pointer finger, and told David and Ken, "You must give your whole heart to Jesus. All for Jesus through Mary." Then in a serious tone she continued, "If you don't want to be a holy priest, you get out now!"

They looked at each other, thinking, "Oh, my gosh! This is serious!"

Father David remarked, "It was a beautiful experience, that Mother Teresa took that opportunity to instill upon us future priests the dire importance of our vocation. All seminarians, and all priests for that matter, should be conscious of the great need for them to be holy, the urgent need for them to live their high calling worthily." Since Mother Teresa is such a credible witness of faith and service, of living her vocation with fidelity, when she speaks, she does so with immense authority.

The Heart of a Generation

Father David Toups considers himself in the heart of the John Paul II generation: "I would say that all of us who have had vocations in about the past twenty years are marked by John Paul's courage. How many times he would remind us to be not afraid, quoting the words of our Lord, giving us courage to stand up for the Gospel of life, giving us courage to proclaim the truth with love to the world. John Paul II was an incredible reminder to us of what it is like to be a disciple."

And John Paul's impact on seminarians is ongoing. Father David adds, "These men that I am training now, the present group of seminarians, the only Pope that they ever knew – until Benedict was elected – was John Paul II. He was the Pope they were born with, and they knew no one else as shepherd. The impact of John Paul II is huge, not only his life and witness, but also his theology (here I am thinking specifically about theology of the body, and his teaching on the priesthood from *Pastores Dabo Vobis)*. I would say that John Paul in his twenty-five-year pontificate shaped the church of the future. He helped redefine the priesthood within the context of the ecclesial tradition that we have inherited as Catholics. He really called us to be who we are supposed to be."

A Question of Character

John Paul II's teaching on priestly character and on the priestly identity became a passion for Father David. In theology, he took this topic as the focus of his doctoral dissertation, and more recently, he published the book *Reclaiming Our Priestly Character.*

He explains, "One of John Paul's points of emphasis was the ontological change that a priest receives during the sacrament of holy orders, enabling him to stand *in persona Christi* [in the person of Christ]." The Holy Father touched on this point in 2003 in his final encyclical letter, *Ecclesia de Eucharistia,* dedicated to discussion of the Holy Eucharist:

> *As I have pointed out on other occasions, the phrase* in persona Christi *"means more than offering 'in the name of' or 'in the place of' Christ.* In persona *means in specific sacramental identification with the eternal High Priest who is the author and principal subject of this sacrifice of his, a sacrifice in which, in truth, nobody can take his place."*[50] *The ministry of priests who have received the sacrament of holy orders, in the economy of salvation chosen by Christ, makes clear that the Eucharist which they celebrate is a gift which radically transcends the power of the assembly and is in any event essential for validly linking the Eucharistic consecration to the sacrifice of the cross and to the Last Supper…This minister is a gift which the assembly receives through episcopal succession going back to the Apostles.*[51]

Father David recalls, "The Holy Father would say over and over when he spoke to priests, 'Be who you are.' Become what you are supposed to be, know who you are as a priest, and live that life, and allow it to invigorate everything that you do. Understand this gift which you have received through the laying on of hands. John Paul II was such a great proponent for the renewal of the priesthood, and I really credit him in a huge way, in a sole way, with the present renewal of the priesthood in the Church, not only in America, please God, but in the world."

The last time Father David saw the Pope was in May of 2004, less than a year before the Pope died. "I had just defended my doctorate," he says, "and my parents were in town for my doctoral defense. A friend of mine who worked in the Vatican got us in for a private audience." In fact, they kind of slipped in to see the Pope, at the end of a group of Polish pilgrims who were going into the apostolic palace.

"I went up to the Holy Father, and looked into those gentle eyes, trapped in an old frail body, and I kissed his ring, the ring of the fisherman, as a sign of my filial love and respect," remembers Father David. Then he handed the Pope a copy of his newly minted doctoral dissertation about the priestly character, the sacerdotal character as the foundation of the priest's life. The Pope nodded, and in his deep Polish accent said, "Good, very good." Then Father David ushered his parents forward, and for a moment his own father and his spiritual father were face-to-face. "I remember seeing tears in my own father's eyes as he met the Holy Father. It was a moment of great joy."

Father David's parents have always been faithful Catholics, embracing everything that the Church teaches, but his mother used to struggle to understand the significance of priestly character, the idea that priests are ontologically changed at ordination, changed at the level of their very being. But some time after Father David's ordination, she told her son that now she knew what that teaching meant. "I didn't believe it until I saw my own son offering the holy sacrifice of the Mass. As I looked at you, I knew it was more than just you, I knew it was Jesus."

As Father David puts it, "Hearing that from my mother just blew my socks off."

He recounts, "I can remember the moment in my own ordination of the laying on of hands – a practice which St. Paul often writes about. The Holy Spirit really marks the soul of the young man at that moment, giving him the power and the authority of Christ, to be exercised in service to the people of God. What a profound gift! As St. John Vianney said, 'If priests understood the gift we received, we would die of fright.'"

Simply Outrageous

"For me as a priest, there is no greater joy than to celebrate Mass, elevating the body and blood of our Lord. For a young man that is discerning the call to the priesthood, it is so common to focus on all the negatives – the things he is giving up: a wife, and children, and a job, and money. But what is gained in return as a spiritual father, as a spouse of the Church, is so beyond our wildest expectations. What an incredible gift it is at the consecration to stand at the altar in the person of Christ and say, "This is my body." And as a believer, to realize what Jesus is doing through me is incredible: when we hear confessions, and we see God transforming souls right before our eyes, and feel the tangible presence of the Holy Spirit in the confessional, when you see Jesus healing souls – and sometimes healing bodies – through the anointing of the sick. In this sense, the priesthood is so far beyond me, David Toups. What we have been called to is so outrageous, really. It's outrageous how much God loves us!"

His Excellency, the Most Reverend Peter Joseph Jugis *is bishop of the Diocese of Charlotte, North Carolina.*

Father David Toups *was ordained a priest in 1997. He formerly was a professor of theology at St. Vincent de Paul regional seminary in Boynton Beach, Florida, before being reassigned to serve as associate director for the United States Conference of Catholic Bishops Secretariat of Clergy, Consecrated Life, and Vocations.*

Chapter 7
ALLELUIA!

Attitude Adjustment

"Alleluia! Praise the Lord! Come on in, come in." With that enthusiastic welcome, I had my first encounter with Father Leonard Reisz down in Owensboro, Kentucky, as he threw open the screen door and waved me in. Father Leonard is thin, wiry, and full of spunk, but you couldn't call him a spring chicken by any stretch of the imagination. He hasn't checked recently whether he is the oldest priest in the diocese, and he's not interested in finding out. It's never a title that anybody gets to hang onto for long.

Some years ago, Father Leonard "retired" and moved out of the rectory into a little house down the street from the church.

When I asked him how he had been spending his time of retirement, he said he has taken up hospital and prison ministry: four or five hospitals, several prisons, and a few nursing homes for good measure. I start to feel worn out, just listening to his schedule. Father Leonard would make the rounds each week, saying Mass, visiting people, and bringing cheer wherever he went.

"You know, for a lot of these people, every day's a bad day," Father Leonard quips. "You wake up in the morning and realize you're still in the slammer. Or in a nursing home you're lonely and sick, and doing anything hurts. Sometimes they set the old ladies up in wheelchairs for Mass, and they just lift them out of bed, and they have bed sores and you see them crying. They're just not in a good state of mind for celebrating the sacrament." So before starting Mass, Father Leonard insists on a period of "attitude adjustment." Everyone has to follow his lead in singing a few songs – "Old MacDonald," "Jingle Bells," or "Rudolph the Red-nosed Reindeer"… the season doesn't really matter. If that doesn't work, then a few jokes might be necessary."

At one nursing home, Father Leonard asked everybody to raise their hands if they wanted to go to heaven. And everyone threw their hands up. Then he asked how many wanted to go today, and all the hands flew down – except for one lady in back with her hand still up…at least until someone beside her leaned over and yelled, "Ethel, is your hearing aid on?"

"Everybody wants to go to heaven, but no one wants to go today!" After Father Leonard sees some smiles and is satisfied that attitudes are sufficiently adjusted, he asks for a moment of silent preparation, so Mass can begin reverently.

Then there are the poor folks in town – someone has to take care of them. So Father Leonard makes a stack of sandwiches for lunch. Anyone that comes to his back door can have a few, as long as they come between eleven o'clock and noon. If anyone is late, they will just have to come back the next day. After all, he can't have people banging on his door all day, and he figures anyone who doesn't show up on time must not be all that hungry after all.

Vine Power

Father Leonard has outlived a passel of popes. But there was always something special about John Paul II, especially his devotion to Christ really present in the Eucharist. "I'll never forget the first time the Pope wrote a letter to us priests on Holy Thursday," says Father Leonard. "Our bishop sent us all a copy, and it really touched me. I read that letter again each year and use it for my prayer."

If you wonder where Father Leonard gets all his enthusiasm, if you wonder how he has kept going through thick and thin, an answer can be found in the theme that runs through all those Holy Thursday letters:

> *Let us rediscover our priesthood in the light of the Eucharist!... Through the centuries, countless priests have found in the Eucharist the consolation promised by Jesus on the evening of the*

Last Supper, the secret to overcoming their solitude, the strength to bear their sufferings, the nourishment to make a new beginning after every discouragement, and the inner energy to bolster their decision to remain faithful.[52]

All alone, one priest can do nothing, but united to Christ, the true vine, he can bear much fruit.

Recently, Father Leonard has been forced to cut back on his work. His heart doctor told him that his old ticker just cannot take the strain. So now he only says Mass at the women's prison and one of the nursing homes – he could not give those places up because the people there need him so badly.

Yet the restricted schedule has not diminished his priestly zeal. A priest's life lived in prayer and sacrifice is a powerful thing. Alongside Christ, he offers his own sufferings and labors to the Father, pleading for the salvation of souls.

Just Like Jesus

Father Jay Toborowsky and Our Lord Jesus Christ have something in common that you might not expect. No, it's not that Father Jay wears sandals, or walks across the country on foot to preach the Gospel. Nor does he have a beard or speak Aramaic. Rather, quite surprisingly, Father Jay also grew up Jewish.

His father's side of the family was Jewish, and his parents were married by a rabbi. When Jay came along two years later, he was raised Jewish, though he quickly notes that he was not a particularly observant Jewish boy. His family was more of the Hanukkah and Yom Kippur crowd, akin to our Christmas-Easter Catholics. Yet, while Jay was still just a boy, around the time he started school, his parents divorced, and his mother took him to live with his grandmother.

Thankfully, Jay always continued to have a good relationship with his father, who lived in the next town over. Being able to see him was never any kind of problem. However, from this point onward, Jay's grandmother started to have a larger influence on his life. All during grade school, while his mother was away for work, his grandmother would watch him. "My grandma was a very faithful, practicing Catholic," he remembers, "so obviously when I was a little kid, she would go to Mass, and I would go with her."

Jay always felt very comfortable at the local church. When he was nine, he joined the Cub Scouts, and through all the years he was involved in scouting, and even later as an adult leader, their meetings were always at the church. "Friends of mine were Catholic, and they all were members of the parish there," he says. "The church was a place that I was very familiar with."

Meeting in the Middle

After graduating from high school, Jay had no clue what he wanted to do with his life; he had never given the matter much thought. However, shortly after graduation, he did some volunteer work for the local elections in the township of Woodridge, New Jersey, helping a candidate running for mayor. When his horse won the race, Jay found himself with a job offer at City Hall. Without any better ideas, he took the job and entered the world of work.

"Here I am, not quite twenty," he remembers. "All my old friends are off at college studying, but I'm working full time. All of a sudden, I start having all these 'grown-up' things to deal with: a medical plan, a pension plan, a prescription plan. That got me to thinking grown-up thoughts. As far as religion goes, I was probably a Deist at best, if you want to call it that, but I started asking myself, 'What do I believe, what do I want to do with my life, and where am I going with it?' That was one of the first steps."

Jay lived about five miles away from City Hall, and halfway between his home and work stood the local parish church. He can't point to any specific moment when he made the decision, but before work began at 8:30 in the morning, he started stopping to visit the church for a while. The process was very natural; he had been familiar with the church most of his life.

Coincidentally, daily Mass was celebrated at the same time in the morning that Jay would stop by, so he started going to daily Mass, just sitting in a pew toward the back for the ceremony. By and by, he started to get the feeling that God was calling him to become Catholic. After reflecting about the idea, he began taking instruction in the faith from a local priest. In September of 1990, he was baptized and entered the Church.

Step by Step

Gradually, Jay started getting involved in the parish. A short time after he entered the church, the old pastor received a new assignment, and a young pastor came in. This new priest was trying to get more young people involved in the parish. Since he saw Jay coming to Mass each day, he asked him whether he would mind being a lector for daily Mass. Jay agreed, and this was the first step in a series of deeper involvements, individually insignificant, but collectively leading in a common direction.

Soon the priest started turning to Jay for more help. "Hey, we're starting a youth group, and I want to get some young adult chaperones – would you be able to help out?"

"No problem."

"Hey, could you help us as an extraordinary minister of communion on Sundays?"

"Sure, why not."

"Before long I was spending more time at the parish," remembers Father Jay. "I was enjoying being involved with the parish, and being a small community, other people started noticing, too. Sometimes others can see signs of a vocation in you before you can see it in yourself. Daily Mass was mostly an older crowd, so when they see a young man coming frequently, they start to wonder."

About this time there was a notice in the parish bulletin about a diocesan "day of reflection" for young men thinking about the priesthood. After wrestling with the idea, Jay summoned up the courage to make the phone call and put his name down for the retreat. A good group showed up on Saturday afternoon, other young guys who were feeling the way Jay did, struggling with what God was asking.

"Coming into the church from the outside, I always thought the priestly vocation was something you were almost born into," laughs Father Jay. "I thought you needed years of Catholic schooling, preparation from childhood. But I spoke to a priest afterward, and told him my situation and that he might think it was weird, but I thought God might be calling me to the priesthood. Then, I bounced the idea off the priest who had baptized me and brought me into the church. I asked him if it was just that I was new and zealous; I asked him if this is something that happens to guys after they come into the church. But he said, 'No, you're mature enough; you're not some impulsive teenager. You would know the difference.' So in both of those cases I was talking to people who said, 'You know I could kind of see a vocation in you,' or, 'I've wondered about it.'"

Then came the last straw. Four times a year, the bishop of the diocese would host an evening of recollection in the next town over, a couple miles away. He would give a talk, celebrate Mass, and hear confessions. So Jay went, determined to speak with the bishop. He waited until he was the last one to go into the confessional, and he told the bishop that he wanted to ask a few questions, the same sort of questions he had asked the priests about discerning a vocation. The bishop was very kind, and afterward Jay sent him a thank-you note. The bishop passed the information on to the vocation director, who suddenly had a big interest in talking with Jay. In August of 1992, Jay was accepted as a seminarian, and entered the college seminary at Seton Hall, later going to study Theology at Mount St. Mary's in Emmitsburg, Maryland. He was ordained in May of 1998.

See You in the Funny Papers

Father Jay's first memory of John Paul II dates from long before his entry into the church. He was a twelve-year-old Jewish boy, sitting in his grandmother's house, in October 1979, when the Pope made his first visit to New York. "At home, my grandmother used to get the paper delivered, the *Sunday Daily News,"* he told me. "Of course, as a kid I loved it because it was wrapped in comics when they first got it. When the Pope's visit was about to happen, the paper had a special insert about the papal visit. I'm sure they had stories and articles, and wonderful things about his life, but what I remember are some pages, almost like what you would see when kids have paper dolls, with illustrations of all the things that the Pope wears: pictures of the Mass vestments, the white cassock and zucchetto, the choir outfit with the cream rochet and red mozetta, the alb and cincture, everything. And there was an explanation of what each was, what it was used for, and why."

"So there I am, twelve years old and Jewish, but fascinated. It was something to see, the vestments and the things that a priest wore. Looking back, I think that these pieces of distinctive attire have a tremendous vocational value. Not that these externals can ever be a reason to become a priest, but because for young boys, you can never underestimate the value of their curiosity about the vestments, sacred vessels, and liturgical items. All those things have deep symbolic meanings, closely related with the priestly identity."

As Father Jay talks, I can't help but remember my own childhood experiences as an altar server, whispering with the other boys in the sacristy before Mass, peeking into drawers and cabinets, looking at the glass cruets and candles, chalices and silver ciboriums, but most of all the thurible for incense – boys are universally attracted by smoke and fire! Few people know this, but years ago altar servers used to be much older. One of the reasons for allowing younger boys to be acolytes was precisely because of the value it has for fostering vocations.

Father Jay continues, "Oddly, there was a time when the attitude in some circles was that if the church wanted to get vocations, then priests should dress like everybody else – 'Let's be relevant and try to blend in.' But the truth is that I was never looking for someone who blended in. If the Pope had come to New York wearing what everybody else wears, I wouldn't have noticed him."

Rome-ward Bound

Of course, as a seminarian, Jay's fascination with the Pope took on entirely different, much deeper dimensions. He started reading the Pope's writings, even using some of them for prayer. During Lent one year, he remembers receiving a booklet of meditations on the Stations of the Cross, based on the Lenten retreat Cardinal Wojtyla gave to the papal household in 1976, shortly before becoming Pope himself. These meditations, published under the title *Sign of Contradiction,* were a profound reflection on the mystery of the cross. Jay was impressed.

When the opportunity came to visit Rome and see the Pope in person, he jumped at the chance. "While I was at Seton Hall, one of the departments was running a study tour of Rome during winter break, geared toward honors students and the classical studies crowd. I certainly wasn't in that category, but many students who had signed up later backed out, and they were looking for people to fill a bunch of empty spots."

So Jay went to his pastor at home to ask for a loan to cover the trip. "I basically sold myself into slavery for the upcoming summer." He remembers telling the priest, "Hey, I need the money now, but in the summer I'll work it off." The pastor was amenable to the suggestion and gave Jay what he needed for the trip.

Jay had heard stories about seminarians attending the Pope's private Mass in the papal apartments, so he started investigating how this was arranged. Eventually, he talked to a Polish priest in the Archdiocese of Newark, the late Monsignor Walter Gorsky, who was reputedly friends with the Pope's secretary, the now Cardinal Stanislaw Dziwisz. Monsignor Gorsky took out a yellow Post-it® note, wrote down a phone number, and said, "Call this number when you get to Rome, and ask for Dziwisz. Tell him that you're a friend of mine, and you wondered if it is possible to come to the morning Mass."

"So here I am thinking, *Who am I to make this call?* First, I didn't realize it was a Vatican extension. I couldn't get it to work from the youth hostel in Rome, and I went to the front desk where they told me that you have to dial the number from a phone booth in the Vatican. So I went to a pay phone in St. Peter's Square, looked up at the papal apartments, and thought to myself, *What am I doing?*

Then, when Monsignor Dziwisz came on the phone, in my best broken Italian, I said, 'There are two of us seminarians here' (I was with a friend from the diocese of Camden) 'and we are going to be in Rome until this day; is there any way that we could come to one of the morning Masses?' And he said, 'Oh, that is very, very difficult...very busy.' But he told me to write a letter with my name and phone number and give it to one of the Swiss Guards at the bronze doors below the papal palace."

Sure enough, four or five days later, the call came: "Be at the bronze doors at 6:40 tomorrow morning."

Beyond the Portal

Jay stood with a small group gathered at bronze doors, shivering a bit, partly from the cool morning air, partly from anticipation. Then a Swiss Guard, thankfully without a spear-like halberd, dressed in a simple blue uniform with tilted beret in place of the showier multi-striped ceremonial outfit, motioned for them to follow, and they entered into the depths of the papal palace.

Each footstep on the mirrorlike marble echoed down the corridor as they continued through the labyrinth of staircases and hallways, past sections of Raphael's renowned loggia decorating the arcaded galleries, through a courtyard and up an elevator until they arrived just outside the doorway of the papal apartments.

The door was closed, so the guard phoned inside. They heard the jingling of keys, the turning of a heavy lock, and the creaking of the door upon its hinges as it swung to reveal the welcoming face of Monsignor Dziwisz. He brought them through a shadowy antechamber where they left their coats, past the massive conference table in the stateroom (after Mass they would return to this room to greet the Pope, and no doubt many have a picture hanging on their wall of themselves with the Pope in that room).

At last, they went around the corner from the big stateroom to the intimate space of the Pope's private chapel. The chapel is simple and elegant, decorated in a more modern style. A large crucifix centered above the altar and tabernacle dominates the view. Slightly lower on the right, beneath one of the arms of the cross, is an icon of the Blessed Virgin Mary – a reproduction of the Black Madonna, Our Lady of Czestochowa, under which title she is hailed as beloved protectress of Poland. The original icon, under the protection of the Pauline monks at Jasna Góra, bears three cuts on its right cheek, said to be from the knife of a desecrator who dropped his blade as the first slashes began to drip blood.

By the time guests arrived for Mass, the Pope already had spent more than an hour in private prayer.

Father Jay describes the scene: "Your first experience is seeing John Paul kneeling at his chair, facing the crucifix and altar in prayer. Instantly, you notice the quiet – and you can hear him breathing, and you can see his shoulders moving as he breathes, and you hear these sighs sometimes. You saw his prayer time before Mass."

This reminds me of the questions about prayer that the Italian journalist, Vittorio Messori, asked John Paul II in *Crossing the Threshold of Hope*. The Holy Father replied to those questions somewhat elusively, aimed as they were at the inner depths of his spiritual life, saying, "You would have to ask the Holy Spirit! The Pope prays as the Holy Spirit permits him to pray." Also, he referenced Romans 8:26: "The Spirit too comes to the aid of our weakness; for we do not know how to pray as we ought, but the Spirit itself intercedes with inexpressible groanings."

Father Jay continues, "Then the Pope stands, and they bring the vestments over to him, and taking each item, he puts them on over his cassock, majestically, an impressive moment. In later years, he needed more help; it was more like helping to dress your grandfather at the end. They had to put the amice on him and help tie it, then the cincture, and he ties the cincture, and as he's vesting someone is straightening out the pleats in his alb and chasuble."

"He went through the Mass carefully, not overly slow, but you could see that he was always conscious about what he was saying. After the reading of the Gospel, you had a couple minutes of silence and then went directly into the liturgy of the Eucharist – no homily or intercessions. Again, after the reception of Communion, there was a time of quiet prayer, before the Pope would stand for the closing prayer… After Mass they would help him remove the vestments from over his white cassock, and he would kneel again to pray his thanksgiving after the Eucharist.

"While he was still praying, they signaled us to leave the room. So when we came into the chapel, the Pope was on his kneeler, and when we left the chapel he was again kneeling in prayer. Then afterward, once they had us all lined up, he came out of the chapel to greet us. In the earlier years he would go around the perimeter of the room, but the last time I saw him, in 2001, he sat in a chair, and we went up to him."

Eventually, Father Jay had the chance to attend the Holy Father's morning Mass on four occasions: the first in 1994 and the last in 2001. "They were powerful encounters; you felt holiness come from him. You knew you were in the presence of God in the room, and John Paul was sort of the filter that you saw the Mass through as he was celebrating it...You can sit through Mass at times, even as a seminarian, where your mind is wandering...you're trying your best to be holy, but you're thinking of classes, you're thinking of papers, of tests, of teachers, you're thinking of everything. But you say to yourself, 'How much does the Pope have to do in his day?' Still, the Eucharist is his focus; he showed us that this is what's most important."

Alleluia!

Of course, a particular incident at one of those Masses is unforgettable, both because it revealed John Paul's human side, and because it nearly gave Father Jay a heart attack.

As he neared the end of theology studies, his entire seminary class, a group of seventeen, planned a trip to Rome around Christmas of 1996. They had been planning the trip for several years, since the start of theology, and they had coaxed Cardinal Hickey of Washington, D.C., into writing a letter on their behalf asking for an invitation to the Pope's morning Mass.

They hadn't received a reply before leaving for Rome, but while they were in St. Peter's Square at the Pope's Wednesday audience, a papal events manager saw their group, and told them that they were expected for the Pope's Mass on December 21, the feast of St. Peter Canisius. But there was one catch: Since they were all seminarians, the Pope would expect them to sing the Mass parts. Of the group, only Father Jay was in the seminary choir.

He was elected cantor by acclamation.

So there he was, standing at the little, modern wrought iron pulpit in the Pope's chapel, his knuckles whitening as he clenched its sides. The Pope watched him from just a few feet away – not to mention the president of South Korea and a handful of other dignitaries in attendance. He sang the responsorial psalm in a simple musical setting without trouble. But as he finished, panic struck.

"I was wondering if the Pope wanted a moment of quiet time before the Gospel. Should I wait, or should I not wait? So I just stopped. Of course, at this point I am right in front of the Pope. He's there with his eyes closed, and I'm watching him and thinking, *What do I do, what do I do, what do I do… what am I doing here?* And sure enough he opens his eyes, looks straight at me and starts humming the tune, 'Alleluia, A-A-LE-LU-IA-A…' Okay! I started singing, 'Alleluia…'

"That instant of eye contact, that moment is burned into my memory, the instant when I am watching the Pope with his eyes closed, and he looks up, opens his eyes, and looks at me. Oh boy!"

After Mass, their group waited together to greet the Pope, and he asked them how long they had until ordination. They replied that deaconate ordinations were in the spring.

"Ah, diaconate, very close," he says and took two more steps. "Priesthood, very close." Before parting, much to Father Jay's relief, he complimented the group, "You sang very well, and in Latin!"

The Next Generation

I asked Father Jay about his perception of the John Paul II generation and its future. "Here was a man," he mused, "who influenced young men, priests, and seminarians just by his actions, just by how he lived. He wasn't doing it to impress us or to recruit us, he was simply being himself, he was being authentic, and that was intensely attractive. We soaked it up; he scattered the seed, and we grew.

"John Paul was a priest no matter where he was; it wasn't just a job for him. That has stuck with me, regardless of what I am doing – if I am in the supermarket, if I am in the confessional, if I am out playing recreational hockey – I am a priest no matter what."

"When John Paul II died they were interviewing all kinds of people around St. Peter's square, and they interviewed some Italian kid who said the Pope never watered down the message. We couldn't always live it, but he never compromised the message, he called us to a higher task and better things.

"A friend of mine was in Rome when the Pope died. He went down to the square, and as an American, he tried to help pilgrims find places to sleep. He said that you haven't lived until you've seen Italian punk rockers sitting in a circle in St. Peter's Square praying the Rosary. You just cannot imagine…the graces started fifteen minutes after John Paul got to heaven.

"What has happened since his death says a lot. It just shows that he wasn't looking for affection and veneration for himself, because it has transferred to Pope Benedict now. No one has said, 'We loved John Paul, but we don't know the new guy.' The criticism was that he was a larger-than-life media figure, he was an actor who was playing this part and it would end with him, but obviously not. Instead, the office and perception of the papacy has been taken to a whole new level. Pope Benedict has just as much of an appeal, and has even larger crowds coming to see him. The John Paul generation understands and has shifted its affection to the new Pope. Perhaps John Paul II uncovered one of the previously unidentified charisms of the office: magnetism. It's only coming out now in the media age."

Father Leonard Reisz *is a priest in the Diocese of Owensboro, Kentucky.*

Father Jay Toborowsky *is parochial vicar of St. Mary's Church in the Diocese of Metuchen, New Jersey.*

Chapter 8
A VOICE IN THE SILENCE

A Special Crop

As Iowa farmer John Hayes penned his handwritten letter to the Pope, he was unsure whether to expect a reply. However, that uncertainty did not trouble him. He wanted the new Pope to know he was welcome in the Hawkeye state, so he sealed his letter in an envelope addressed to the Vatican and dropped it in the mail.

Sometimes small decisions have big consequences.

Mr. Hayes was stunned not only to receive a reply, but also to have the Pope accept his invitation. John Paul II added a brief stop in Iowa to the itinerary of his first apostolic visit to the United States. His helicopter would touch down in

Iowa just two days after his scheduled address at the United Nations headquarters in New York.[53]

This unexpected alteration created a great deal of excitement for organizers in Des Moines, who had only a few weeks to complete preparations. Huge crowds were expected to attend the Pope's Mass. As a venue, Living History Farms, a 500-acre outdoor agricultural museum on the west side of Des Moines, was chosen. The farm, which traces the progress of Midwestern agricultural life from the arrival of the first settlers to the modern era, offered a picturesque backdrop for the Pope's visit.

Darwin Thede, manager for the farm's "pioneer area" and resident on the grounds from 1970-1987, was involved in the preparations. He remembers helicopters flying over the farm in the days before the Pope's arrival, presumably planning for traffic flow and evacuation routes. On the farm's grounds, an outdoor altar was constructed in the pasture behind an 1870s brick barn and farmstead. After the visit, Darwin remembers with humor, a small nondenominational chapel was erected on the site. However, the undertaking was something of a fiasco. First, the unfinished structure collapsed in a windstorm. Then, after hosting its first wedding, the second structure caught fire and burned to the ground. The present chapel is attempt number three.

The day of October 4, 1979, started out cool and cloudy, with an overcast sky. But as the hour of the Pope's arrival approached, the weather cleared up and the clouds melted beneath warm sunshine. A crowd had started to gather on the previous day when parish groups prepared to camp out overnight. On the day itself, many travelers left their cars at a great distance and walked up to ten or twelve miles; others rode bicycles to reach the grounds. The crowd – a mixture of families, older folks, and young people – represented a cross section of America's heartland.

When the awaited moment finally came, Darwin was on site as part of an eight-man work team. He was only a short distance away from the altar during the Pope's homily, and he remembers that the Pope spoke about agriculture and the role of farmers. The Holy Father also had a deeper spiritual point to convey:

> *Here in the heartland of America, in the middle of bountiful fields at harvest time, I come to celebrate the Eucharist… Farmers everywhere provide bread for all humanity, but it is Christ alone who is the bread of life. He alone satisfies the deepest hunger of humanity… While we are mindful of the physical hunger of millions of our brothers and sisters on all continents, at this Eucharist we are reminded that the deepest hunger lies in the human soul. Even if all the physical hunger of the world were satisfied, even if everyone who is hungry were fed…the deepest hunger of man would still exist… Therefore, I say: Come, all of you, to Christ. He is the bread of life. Come to Christ, and you will never be hungry again.*[54]

After the Mass ended and the crowd dispersed, Darwin sat down to satisfy his own hunger, and started cooking supper at the fireplace of an 1850's farmstead. Meanwhile, a few remaining secret service agents passed by the farmstead. They had been on hand to oversee security and to ensure the Holy Father's safety. One of them stopped beside Darwin and voiced his amazement about the day's event.

The 350,000-strong crowd was larger than any gathered in the history of Iowa, and there had been fears about what could happen in a gathering of such massive size. Event managers warned that in all likelihood several people in the crowd would die of heart attacks, that there would be pickpockets, possibly fights, and even an unexpected baby delivery or two.

But in the secret service agent's opinion, something about this crowd had been different. He couldn't put his finger on it, but for some reason the gathering had been the easiest he had ever handled.

That record-breaking crowd had reason to be different. John Paul had sown the seeds of the Gospel amid the cornfields of Iowa, and that crowd was his special crop.

Searching for Sioux City

Years later, in a city far from the fields of Iowa, someone else remembered that October day of '79. As his finger covered the small map dot labeled "Des Moines," John Paul II blurted out to the bishop beside him, "I was there!" However, he still couldn't locate the smaller metropolis of Sioux City.

"It was hilarious," Cardinal Daniel DiNardo remembers. "He was trying to find where Sioux City, Iowa, was on the map." This was in 1998, about a year after DiNardo became bishop of Sioux City. The Pope remembered saying Mass in a big cornfield outside Des Moines, but he still couldn't pick out Sioux City, located about 150 miles northwest.

"I showed him where Sioux City was, and we had a nice discussion about rural dioceses," DiNardo says. "We were discussing multiple things, about rural dioceses and matters of that sort – this was back when the Pope was still rather healthy and very much alert as to what was going on. But what I recall most of all is that at the end of the meeting, right before he buzzed for the photographer to come in, he said, 'Just remember, it's always about the human person.' That was a line I thought was magnificent."

In subsequent years, DiNardo has had many opportunities to reflect on that nugget of wisdom, and he has striven to place concern for the human person at the center of his ministry.

In 2007, when the fifty-eight-year-old Archbishop of Galveston-Houston became the first cardinal in the history of Texas, he brought with him many lessons learned from John Paul II, even as he prepared to place his talents at the disposal of Peter's latest successor. DiNardo embraced his new role with a request to his flock: "I ask all members of this local church, and all the people of goodwill here, to pray for me and ask the Lord to help me as I continue to shepherd this local archdiocese and, at the same time, assume the title that increases my responsibility to work on behalf of the whole church and collaborate with the Holy Father in his immense responsibility as Pope."[55]

Nothing Fuzzy at All

Through his years as a priest and bishop, DiNardo watched with interest as the younger generation responded to John Paul II. I asked the cardinal about his perspective as to the reality of a "John Paul II generation."

"There's certainly a truth to it," Cardinal DiNardo said, "particularly with a whole group of priests who came to the seminary, I would say, in the late '80s after he had been Pope about ten years. I noticed it when I was working in Rome, among some of the new students coming into the North American College where I taught the first year methodology seminar for a couple of years. I noticed a difference coming at that point, and certainly it was true through the '90s.

"That was when we were also watching, really, a major transition even in seminaries. My seminary was the North American College in Rome where I studied theology, and I noticed a difference already in the '80s but really full-blown by the 1990s. I believe that it was a number of things. It was the young people responding, sometimes to World Youth Days, sometimes to other things the Pope had done."

John Paul had an incredible sense of vitality and a zest for life that resonated with the young and young at heart. DiNardo observes, "Even as he got older and couldn't do as much, I remember seeing pictures of him where he couldn't do the heavy skiing he did before, but he was still on skis! Those are the kind of things that as a young man and a young priest that he found so invigorating, and I think that was a strong point, and a cause of the initial enthusiastic response to him. Most of the young people had to go deeper, though, and try to understand what he was saying, and that challenged them, and I think they liked that because he never talked down to them, he challenged them directly. He had fun with them, and then he hit them square, which was the normal way he did it."

"He would say 'Hey, this is what I am going to tell you, this is what the faith thinks, and I'm not going to sugarcoat it, but I am also going to tell you that it's an invigorating life.' And I think young people responded. Particularly given that the post-Vatican II church seemed to be at times – and this is exaggerated at times and I don't mean to overdraw it – seemed to be either hesitating about its identity or fuzzy. Nothing was fuzzy with John Paul II."

The Quiet Storm

This influence was by no means restricted to priests and seminarians. In the culture at large, John Paul II left his mark. "I know families from all over the country in the various places that I have been, and they always name one of their kids John Paul. One of the reasons for doing it is that they have such affection for John Paul, and they saw that in their own lives he was a most engaging man. They were young people who loved the priesthood but who had no intention of ever being priests, but who in their lives represent a small but significant leaven for the culture. John Paul II certainly saw the difficulties of the culture and he occasionally thought that the culture was hostile, but he also thought that the culture could be taken by a quiet storm which was the love of Jesus in the hearts of those who witness to him in a variety of professions and situations in life.

"Many leaders would look to young people and ask them to aspire, but they never challenged young people the same way that Pope John Paul II did. In fact, when the Pope died, the incredible number of young people who came to Rome frequently astounded commentators. But if you had been following all along the relationship between the Holy Father and young people, it wasn't surprising at all. It made perfect sense."

As opposed to the glitz and glamour of Hollywood, where camera magic, makeup, and plastic surgery attempt to pass off illusion as reality, John Paul II's approach was refreshing. Young people could sense almost instinctively that he was a man without duplicity – someone they could trust to speak the truth.

"The Holy Father was true to himself," DiNardo says, "in that, being a vigorous young Pope in 1978 and '79, a guy who went skiing, who liked the outdoors and that sort of thing, as he aged he never hid it. In a culture that likes to deal in, as I would call it, both material and spiritual cosmetics, the Holy Father was never cosmetic about himself."

DiNardo recounts one incident which occurred at a dinner in 1998 or 1999 with the Holy Father that typifies the Holy Father's approach. "I remember sitting next to Bishop Dziwisz, as one of the youngest bishops at the dinner, and talking with him. But at one point, one of the archbishops – I won't say who – told the Holy Father, 'We want to see you around for a long time; maybe you should slow down.' The Pope just looked at him and said, 'Ahh, if I drop, I drop.' There were no cosmetics with the Pope. He'd say, 'If I look bad, then I'll just have to look bad.' He did not try to hide it.

"I think for numerous young people that was a sign of authenticity, a sign that whatever the circumstances, we live our life in Christ. The Pope's challenge to young people was not something he didn't also respond to himself. I think amongst heavy world leaders, John Paul II was the most inspiring to them."

Teaching by Example

I asked Cardinal DiNardo what lesson John Paul had for young people about prayer. "Well," he said, "at times he would speak to the youth about the need for times of silence and prayer, as he challenged them also to live lives of integrity, morality, and purity, and to encounter the Lord Jesus. But a large part of what he did was through example. There are so many pictures and so many people who remember him being himself at prayer. There's no better way; that's how you tell people.

"In addition to the large-scale liturgies that he did, the Pope could also be seen in prayer, in quiet, and at lengths, so that his ability to speak about prayer came from deep resources, from the practice of it. I think his marvelous document, written a year or two before he died, *Ecclesia de Eucharistia*, was a beautiful statement on the centrality of the Eucharist and the value of our visits to the Blessed Sacrament in prayer and adoration. Then our outreach is not out of pure philanthropy, as it were, but out of the deep abiding sense of God's presence with us that's shared with others. The Pope had a real strategy, which was basically the strategy of the Gospel, and he was able to bring that to young people."

Learn to Listen

Cardinal DiNardo also has some words of guidance for young people who are discerning God's call. "My first advice," he says, "would be to make sure that you stay close to the Holy Eucharist and to the liturgy. That is very, very important. Regular, consistent, and prayerful participation in the liturgy and in the Eucharist, visits to the Eucharist, keeping to one side the 'energy of acceptance' of the Virgin Mary, and then, and again I'm going to say it in a crass way, although it should be said more subtly, learn in your prayer to shut up! It is pretty important. The contemplative gaze on the face of Jesus will do far more than the 'let's put things in order…

I do this first, and then this and this' because the Lord will eventually show you the way – as you mentioned earlier about the noise, some of the noise is outside, but there is occasional noise inside. That may be far more difficult to break down. But contemplative prayer is important; I also think that while you are doing that that some people, especially young people, can really understand that."

"Once that is in place, make sure you are doing some form of action or outreach to the poor. That acts as a clarifying agent, particularly to occasionally hopelessly romantic young people. When you roll up your sleeves and realize that things are a little messier than you thought, but nonetheless you can still embrace the Lord, then you have reached a second level of maturity, and the Lord will show you the way. Obviously, you need to talk to some people – a good priest, a spiritual director, someone who is trustworthy who can help you. The Father never said through his Son Jesus that when he calls, he is going to call you so apocalyptically alone that you're going to have the experience of St. Paul. That is rare. Most people don't have that Pauline experience.

"People often ask me what happened in terms of my becoming a priest, and I say that I never had any apocalyptic visions, and I never had any so called absolute moments. But the one thing that was a gift given to me through a couple of great schools of nuns was love for the liturgy. If one loves the liturgy and is attentive to the liturgy, it is amazing how the liturgy teaches without necessarily teaching classroom-wise.

The liturgy is always teaching, but it is so quiet; it teaches through word, gesture, and sacrament. If you love the liturgy, you will get attached to the Word of God, and the Word of God will get through the noise."

Silencing the Noise

Eighteen-year-old Anthony Denton had just such an experience of the Lord's voice piercing through the chaos of his life. As he was considering going on a "silent retreat," he was skeptical about whether anyone could actually be quiet for three whole days. In that respect, he was a typical Australian lad. Every moment of the day was saturated with noise: telephone, television, radio, and music. When the noise wasn't external, the chaos continued inside, with music and memories that kept running like hamsters on wheels.

"I was interested in rock music myself," Father Anthony says. "I could never really play anything like guitar, but I enjoyed it."

At his college, there were plenty of opportunities for such enjoyment. With parties, concerts, and pub nights, there was something going on virtually all week. "There was a real party atmosphere," he says, "but at the same time I must have been really searching."

Father Anthony came from a Catholic family that went to church on Sunday and prayed, and he thought he could do that and still live a life at the university which wasn't really a Christian life. However, everything changed in an unexpected way.

"I went on this retreat, and it was an amazing experience," he remembers. "It was like a conversion experience. In the presence of the Blessed Sacrament, with the prayers of the church and talks given by this very good young priest, I immediately knew that I wanted to change my life and live for God."

That experience is the first instance Father Anthony points to as the beginning of his call. "At first, it was just this idea of conversion – that whatever I wanted to do, I wanted to serve God. But pretty much at the same time I thought that obviously the way to do that would be to be a priest."

He remarks with humor about the significance of that chance for quiet reflection, and how different it was from his daily experience. "For me, this retreat was a big contrast with going to university pub nights and concerts. Really, the only other experience of silence I had during that stage was Mass on Sundays – for the small amount of silence you can get in Mass these days. So the thought of a silent retreat was quite shocking. In fact, I remember thinking about not going for that reason, because how could you have silence for that long?"

That is the attitude that Father Anthony Denton now commonly experiences in his position as vocations director for the Archdiocese of Melbourne, Australia. Now he is in charge of directing the same retreat he once hesitantly attended. When I spoke with him, he had just printed flyers for the upcoming retreat – deliberately avoiding the word "silent" to keep from spooking anyone. Now they simply label it as a "Retreat for Young Men."

"I think that silence is crucial to the discernment process and to doing a serious retreat," Father Anthony says. "It is better to explain why it is silent after they arrive, otherwise they will decide not to come because of the silence. I really think they can't discern without silence."

John Paul II addressed the same point to Australians in his document *Ecclesia in Oceania.* Coincidentally, that document speaks about a topic of great importance to Father Anthony, the need for silence and prayer.

> *The frenetic activity of modern life with all its pressures makes it indispensable that Christians seek prayerful silence and contemplation as both conditions for and expressions of a vibrant faith. When God is no longer at the center of human life, then life itself becomes empty and meaningless…*[56] *Jesus himself often "went off to a lonely place and prayed there…"*[57] *Jesus' prayer is our example, especially when we are caught up in the tensions and responsibilities of daily life.*[58]

Father Anthony experienced the wisdom of the Holy Father's insight. He recounts, "When I was on that first retreat, there were about twelve young men attending. It was held on a country property run by a religious order, and it wasn't what I had expected. I had never before experienced such peace and calm – so much so that I really didn't want the retreat to end. It was only for about three or four days, but if I could put down one thing that definitely influenced my vocation, it would be that. It enabled me to listen beyond all the noise of the world to God speaking in my heart."

Someone Close to Us

Father Anthony fits squarely in the midst of the John Paul II generation. He entered the seminary in 1995 and was ordained in 2002. During the progression of his seminary years, Father Anthony developed an increasing love for the Holy Father, and he treasures memories of personal contacts with him.

"Certainly," Father Anthony says, "John Paul's influence on my vocation was both personal – in the sense of the example of his life – and intellectual – because of the great amount of documents and encyclicals he wrote which were right during the time of my formation. His influence was an all embracing influence."

Memories of his providential meetings with John Paul II helped Father Anthony persevere through difficult moments in his seminary years.

"I have been very lucky," he mentions, and then promptly corrects himself: "However, I shouldn't say 'lucky' at all. I am convinced from all the things in my life that meeting John

Paul II was part of God's providence, part of his plan. As you progress toward the priesthood, there are lots of things that sustain you. I remember once a friend saying to me before I was ordained – when I was having some doubts about becoming a priest, 'I can't understand how you can even be tempted to doubt after all the experiences you have had.' That brought me back to reality."

Father Anthony's first encounter was on a pilgrimage just prior to entering the seminary. However, there were many more opportunities to be near the Pope when Archbishop Pell (now Cardinal Archbishop of Sydney) sent him to study at the Pontifical Urban College in Rome.

"I had four years in Rome between 1998 and 2002," Father Anthony says, "and I stopped ordering the photos after I had met the Pope seven or eight times. [The opportunities] were partly on account of being an Australian in Rome during the preparation of the Jubilee. Lots of events were organized regionally according to continent, and as for the continent of Oceania, only a few seminarians in Rome came under that category. So, in 1998, when we had the Synod for Oceania, they needed everyone to have enough seminarians to serve the opening and closing Masses with the Pope."

Yet even excluding special events, there were many "ordinary" opportunities for Father Anthony to see the Pope. The college where he resided was located on Rome's Janiculum Hill, directly across from the Vatican, and this afforded a unique opportunity.

"We would go up to the roof which is level to the top floor of the apostolic palace," he recalls, "and we would listen to the Pope's Sunday Angelus as he led it from his window."

The audio equipment and PA system in St. Peter's Square had been improved in preparation for the Jubilee Year, so Father Anthony and his rooftop companions could hear every word the Pope said. With binoculars they could look through the Pope's window and see the bookshelves on the back wall of his study.

"Only when I reflect and remember things," says Father Anthony, "do I realize how amazing it was. I went to every canonization and beatification that I could. From all the papal events I have kept the little booklets; I must have about fifty or sixty. I felt like I knew Pope John Paul II because I saw him all the time."

When the time came for Father Anthony's ordination to the diaconate, April 28, 2001, a special opportunity arose. "Archbishop Pell wrote a letter asking for my family to have an audience with the Pope. The week before my diaconate ordination, I got to present my family to the Pope in St. Peter's Square during a general audience, and then on Monday morning, when they were due to leave, we got a phone call from the Pope's secretary, Bishop Dziwisz, saying that if we were at the bronze doors in the morning, we could attend a private audience. It was extraordinary, an amazing grace. We all met the Pope one-on-one. I am one of nine children, and all were there, except for two of my sisters [who were expecting babies at the time]."

That meeting was a turning point in the life of Father Anthony's younger brother. "My younger brother, who is now a seminarian, says that meeting with Pope John Paul was pivotal for him in his own vocation. It was a great and humbling experience to have my brother enter the seminary."

As Father Anthony's period of study in Rome neared its end, and the time for his priestly ordination approached, the Pope left him one last gift. "I was able to be deacon at a private Mass in the Holy Father's chapel," Father Anthony says. "I stood next to the Pope and held up the chalice at the end of the Eucharistic prayer. It is somewhat hard to describe, almost a mystical experience. At the end of the Mass, Bishop Dziwisz came up to me and gave me kind of a compliment, saying that he could see I knew what I was doing. Then he said that the Holy Father would like me to have something, and he handed me the corporal, pall, and purifier which the Pope had used at that Mass."

Father Anthony proudly considers those items to be second-class relics.

John Paul's Legacy

I asked Father Anthony for his perspective about the effect John Paul has had on the groups of seminarians entering in the several years before and after his death. "I think all of them have in some way been influenced by John Paul," he says. "Certainly, following John Paul II's death in 2005, we had a big influx of calls and inquiries. In terms of an attitude among seminarians, I think this is where World Youth Day comes into it. We had a meeting at the seminary to work out how the seminarians would participate in the activities surrounding World Youth Day 2008 in Sydney. The auxiliary bishop asked the group of seminarians: "Who would say that World Youth Day had an influence on your vocation?" Out of the group of about fifty – the majority from Melbourne, but some from the surrounding dioceses as well – somewhere from a third to a half put their hands up. In that sense, World Youth Day, which is one of the great hallmarks of Pope John Paul II, has had a continuing influence.

"The challenge issued to young people at World Youth Day is always the same: the challenge to be faithful to Christ. That has definitely influenced these young men. If they haven't heard it from John Paul II, they've heard it from priests or bishops who in turn got it from the Pope. In particular, here in Melbourne, young people have heard that message from Cardinal Pell, who was the archbishop of Melbourne for five years before being taken to Sydney, and from his successor our present Archbishop Hart. Both of them have given strong leadership, and both were encouraged by the call of John Paul II and have then passed that message on."

Now, Father Anthony himself is conscious of being one more link in that chain. As he fulfills his day-to-day ministry in the Archdiocese of Melbourne, he passes on the spirit and message of John Paul II to a new generation of young people. That spirit is ever ancient and ever new, shared by the great saints of old and the great saints to come. It lives on in the hearts of those who burn with love for Christ.

HIS EMINENCE, DANIEL NICHOLAS CARDINAL DINARDO, *shepherds the Archdiocese of Galveston-Houston, Texas.*

FATHER ANTHONY DENTON, *ordained in 2002, is vocation director for the Archdiocese of Melbourne, Australia.*

ENDNOTES

1. John Paul II, "Message for the 18th World Youth Day," April 13, 2003.
2. RSV Galatians 2:20.
3. NJB Luke 19:5.
4. NJB Luke 22:61.
5. NJB Mark 10:21.
6. John Paul II, "Message to the Youth of the Word on the Occasion of the 20th World Youth Day," August 6, 2004.
7. John Paul II, *Rise, Let Us Be on Our Way* (New York: Warner Books, 2004), p.12.
8. John Paul II, "Homily at the Liturgy of the Word at the McNichols Sports Arena of Denver," August 14, 1993, 1.
9. John Paul II, "Address at Papal Welcoming Ceremony in the Mile High Stadium of Denver," August 12, 1993, 3.
10. Ibid., 5.
11. Cfr. Rom 1:16.
12. Cfr. Matth 10:27.
13. Mt 22:9.
14. John Paul II, "Homily at the Eucharistic Celebration at the Chery Creek State Park of Denver," Solemnity of the Assumption of the Blessed Virgin Mary, August 15, 1993, 6.
15. George Weigel, *Witness to Hope* (New York: HaperCollins, 1999), 282.
16. Pope John Paul II, "Meditation from the Policlinico Gemelli to the Italian Bishops," Insegnamenti, XVII, 1 [1994], 1061.
17. Cardinal Angelo Sodano, "Announcement Made By Cardinal Angelo Sodano Secretary of State at the End of the Mass Presided Over by the Holy Father at Fatima," May 13, 2000.
18. John Paul II, *Rise, Let Us Be on Our Way* (New York: Warner Books, 2004), 66.
19. John Paul II, *Rosarium Virginis Mariae,* 36.
20. cf. *Rosarium Virginis Mariae,* 15.
21. John Paul II, "Message of the Holy Father John Paul II for the 18th World Youth Day," March 8, 2003, 3-4.
22. John Paul II, Homily at Saint Peter's Basilica, October 22, 1978, 5.
23. John Paul II, "Homily at the Liturgy of Vespers at the Chapel of Saint Joseph's Seminary, Yonkers, New York," October 6, 1995.
24. John Paul II, "Homily at the Eucharistic Celebration for the Young People at Central Park, New York," October 7, 1995.
25. Ibid.
26. "Prayer for Asking Graces Through the Intercession of the Servant of God the Pope John Paul II, " with ecclesiastical approval of Cardinal Camillo Ruini, the Holy Father's Vicar General for the Diocese of Rome.
27. Acts 19: 11-12.

28. Cardinal Stanislaw Dziwisz, *A Life With Karol:My Forty-Year Friendship with the Man Who Became Pope* (New York: Doubleday, 2008), 42-43.
29. cf. *Salvifici doloris*, 17-18.
30. Lk 9:23.
31. cf. 1 Cor 1: 22-25.
32. Gal 2:20.
33. John Paul II, "Message to the Youth of the World on the Occasion of the XVI World Youth Day", February 14, 2001, 2-4.
34. John Paul II, *Salvifici doloris,* February 11, 1984, 26.
35. John Paul II, "Letter to Priests for Holy Thursday 1998," March 25, 1998, 7.
36. cf. 1 Cor 4:1.
37. John Paul II, "Omelia di Giovanni Paolo II per Santa Messa per l'Ordinazione di 74 Nuovi Sacerdoti," June 12, 1983, author's own translation.
38. John Paul II, *Rise, Let Us Be on Our Way* (New York: Warner Books, 2004), 9.
39. Ibid., 17.
40. John Paul II, Mane Nobiscum Domine, 5, 29.
41. John Paul II, "Homily on St. Francis of Assisi at Eucharistic Concelebration at the Franciscan Shrine of La Verna," September 17, 1993, digitally provided by CatholicCulture.org.
42. cf. 1 Cor 7:34.
43. John Paul II, *Vita Consecrata*, 1.
44. John Paul II, Address during the Vigil of Prayer with the Young People at Cherry Creek State Park, Denver," August 14, 1993.
45. John Paul II, "Testament of the Holy Father John Paul II."
46. George Weigel, *Witness to Hope*, 513, 566.
47. John Paul II, "Address to the Pilgrims Who Had Come to Rome for the Beatification of Mother Teresa," October 20, 2003.
48. Ibid.
49. John Paul II, "Homily at Beatification of Mother Teresa of Calcutta," October 19, 2003.
50. John Paul II, *Dominicae Cenae* (24 February 1980), 8: AAS 72 (1980), 128-129.
51. John Paul II, *Ecclesia de Eucharistia*, April 17, 2003, 29.
52. John Paul II, "Letter to Priests for Holy Thursday 2000."
53. George Weigel, *Witness to Hope* (New York: HaperCollins, 1999), 351.
54. John Paul II, *The Pope Speaks to the American Church* (San Francisco: HarperSanFrancisco, 1992), 61-64.
55. October 17, 2007, Archbishop Daniel N. DiNardo of Galveston-Houston was elevated to cardinal on Wednesday, KPRC Local 2 report.
56. Cf. Propositio 21.
57. Mk 1:35.
58. John Paul II, *Ecclesia in Oceania*, no. 37.

ABOUT THE ILLUSTRATOR

Mimi Sternhagen is a teacher and an illustrator whose artwork embellishes the publications of several Catholic print houses. She and her husband reside in rural northern California. Their three sons are Brothers with the Legionaries of Christ, and their two daughters are discerning vocations to the consecrated life.

Made in the USA
Lexington, KY
07 April 2011